BREAKING MURPHY'S PROMISE

HOW DEMOCRATS ABANDONED GRANDMA

GEORGE COLEMAN CONRAD

THIS BOOK IS DEDICATED TO:

GRACE SWANEY MURPHY

and

My Mother,
ADDAMAE MURPHY CONRAD

My Father,
CHESTER SAMUEL CONRAD, Sr.

CHAPTER 1

INTRODUCING MURPHY

Grace Maude Swaney was a proud American citizen. Her great grandfather, James John Swaney, was born in Ireland in 1797. He immigrated to the United States via New York City. The Swaney family settled in Pennsylvania. They became farmers.

Grace was born on March 7, 1890 in western Pennsylvania near the town of Fairchance. She died in Fairmont, West Virginia on June 2, 1974 at age 84. She was quite a lady. And she was my Grandma.

She was the daughter of James Brownfield Swaney and Hannah McFadden Swaney. She grew up in a large family. She was the 7th of 13 children. Her childhood was filled with hard chores and emotional hardships. Sister Ellie lived only six weeks and died of typhoid fever. Education was provided in a one-room schoolhouse. Grandma never attended college but must have had a pretty good education. She became a teacher and would later teach at the same schoolhouse where she had attended as a child. Somewhere along the way she gained a lot of common sense and wisdom.

She fell in love when she met her future husband, Walter Coleman Murphy. He was a railroad man, but far from a railroad tycoon. The train life took him to many places. One of those places was Fairchance where he met and fell in love with Grace. They married in 1913 and moved to Fairmont, West Virginia. Fairmont is the very center of the bituminous Coal Fields of Appalachia. Grace Maude Swaney thereby became Grace Swaney Murphy.

Walter Coleman Murphy was my Grandpap. He was born in the backwoods of Marion County, West Virginia on May 3, 1883. Fairmont is the county seat of Marion County. When he was born, the Murphy family had called Marion County home for at least two generations. The Murphy homestead was located beside a small watercourse called Mud Lick Run.

Grandpap Murphy spent several years of his youth in the United States Army. He was posted to Fort Brown in Brownsville, Texas. The Army at Fort Brown patrolled the Mexican border and chased bandits back into Mexico in order to secure America's interests. By 1911 President William Howard Taft had placed 30,000 troops at the border. After his stint in the Army in service to his country Grandpap joined the railroad and worked there for the remainder of his working life.

I have a fond but hazy memory of Grandpap Murphy. I do remember well the two disarmed mortar shells that he brought back home after his military service. They had a prominent place in our home as bookends beside the fireplace. And I do remember that he was very proud of having attained the 32nd degree in the Masonic Temple. That required a good memory and a lot of dedication to principle. He died in 1954 when I was 9 years old. And I remember that he was buried wearing his Masonic apron.

Walter and Grace had two children. The youngest was my Uncle Jake, born in 1916. The firstborn in 1915 was Addamae. Addamae was my Mother. Walter and Grace gave me many gifts, but their gift of my Mother was the greatest gift of all.

My Mother and my Grandma taught me a lot and shaped my life. They taught me to tell the truth and to be responsible for everything that I do. They taught me the value of hard work. They taught me that I was very lucky to be born into this great country. And they taught me their politics. Grandma and Mother were both lifelong Democrats.

Grandma Murphy had grit and would withstand the many challenges of her childhood and adult life with strength and determination, despite the many hard times that she faced. And, in her lifetime she experienced changes in America that, to understate the matter, were simply amazing.

To better understand the transformation of America that Grandma Murphy witnessed and was a part of, I have attempted to tell that story in three separate chapters: roughly her childhood; her adult life; and, her later years. After that we will finally get to Murphy's

Promise, and the significance of that promise. You have my word on that.

So, now that you have met Murphy, let's proceed with her story.

CHAPTER 2

MURPHY'S FORMATIVE YEARS

Grace Maude Swaney grew up about 60 miles southeast of Pittsburgh, living on a small farm in western Pennsylvania, near a small borough known as Fairchance. Her formative years occurred in the last decade of the 19th century and the first decade of the 20th. Her Mother and Father had 13 children and one died of typhoid fever in infancy. The remaining 14 members of her immediate family would have had a hard life.

The blessing of living on a farm was that you could grow most of your own food, so the family would not starve to death. That required everyone to pitch-in and do a fair share of the work required on a farm. And that was a lot of work. The cows had to be milked, the butter had to be churned. The small game rabbits and squirrels had to be hunted by the men folk and cleaned and prepared for cooking by the females. The crops had to be planted and harvested and the vegetables and berries had to be canned.

There were no government poverty programs like social welfare and food stamps. And in relation to today's understanding of what poverty really is, there is a stark difference between then and now. Grace's

Father was a farmer, so he received no wage for his work. If he had been a coal miner, like many of his neighbors, he would have earned about $2 for a 12-hour work day and worked 6 days a week for 52 weeks a year. That is a hard life. The annual income for that labor would be about $625. Because of inflation that would equate to $16,270 in 2020 dollars. Today a family of 14 is considered by government standards to be living in poverty with an annual income of $71,000.

The farmhouse would have several bedrooms to accommodate all those kids. No one but the parents had a separate room. Sleeping three or four to a room was common on the farm.

During Grace's elementary school years, the kitchen would have had a stove but no oven. There would be no refrigeration inside, only an outside cooling house, built over a small stream flowing nearby. Another outhouse would serve as the family toilet. Water for cooking and cleaning was supplied from the well.

There was no electricity. Half of the homes in the United States did not have electric power until 1925. Lighting was provided by kerosene lanterns.

Communication occurred by talking to each other and by writing letters. Grace learned to read and write in a one-room school house. She must have been a pretty good student to pass the 1912 eighth grade final exam. Google it and see if you could pass. By the age of 20 she was the teacher at that same schoolhouse.

Childhood games were simple and played with others. Tag and Leap Frog and Ring Around the Rosie were popular and required no money. The daring kids would be drawn to a game called Mumble-de-Peg. The big blade of a pocket knife would be drawn fully open. The game was played by placing the point of the knife blade first on the palm of the hand, then in turn on the back of the hand, the elbow, the fist, and the knee. From each position the knife would be skillfully flipped to stick the blade into the ground. When the knife did not stick, you lost your turn. Grace's Mother would not have liked that game very much.

Grace's favorite childhood toy would have been a doll. The 1900 Sears, Roebuck and Co. catalog was filled with dolls and doll furniture and doll costumes. But those were unavailable to a poor farm family. Her doll would have been homemade. Another favorite toy at that time was the Teddy Bear. The story was widespread that in 1902 President Teddy Roosevelt went hunting for black bear but chose not to shoot one. That story resulted in the invention of the Teddy Bear that the Sears catalog featured in 1907. As a teenager at that time I doubt that Grace Swaney would have been much interested in wanting a Teddy Bear.

Travel was done mostly by walking. The family would have had a farm horse or two, a farm wagon, and maybe a buggy to hitch the horse to. Everyone was fascinated by the railroad and would delight in getting a ride on rare occasions. In what little spare time they had, teenagers liked to hang out by the Fairchance train depot.

Group music and singing were experienced at church by singing hymns accompanied by a church organ or piano. The Swaney's were Methodists and attended church as a family each Sunday. Sunday was a day off from school and from most chores. The only store-bought musical instrument at home would have been a harmonica, for the family certainly could not afford a piano. The kid's most popular musical instrument would have been a Kazoo. The Kazoo was a homemade percussion instrument that you hummed into. It was made by placing tissue paper over a comb. Humming different syllables into it would make different sounds, and increasing the airflow resulted in a louder tone.

Evenings were spent at home talking and telling stories. Reading by lantern light was a strain on the eyes but provided endless hours of escape from the drudgery of farm life by entering the world of imagination.

When Grace was a small child, she would be entertained by the Hans Christian Andersen tales of *The Little Mermaid* and *The Ugly Duckling*. As a teen she would have been enthralled by the exploits of *The Three Musketeers* and *Robinson Crusoe*.

Grace's life on the family farm had provided a most-challenging but valuable life experience. She had deeply learned the values of hard work and teamwork and education and perseverance that would sustain her throughout her life.

Each day that we awake, each of us is the evolving product of our life experience.

Grace Maude Swaney's formative years came to an end when she met and married Walter Coleman Murphy in Fairchance, Pennsylvania. She then took the train about 50 miles south with her husband to begin a new chapter in her life in the bustling little city of Fairmont, West Virginia in 1913, as Grace Swaney Murphy, a married woman, age 23.

CHAPTER 3

MURPHY'S MIDDLE YEARS

The Murphy family lived at 620 Maryland Avenue on the East Side of Fairmont, West Virginia. Fairmont is located about 30 miles south of the Pennsylvania border, where the Mason-Dixon line defines the northernmost point of America's South. The small city developed around the point where the Tygart Valley River and the West Fork River come together to form the Monongahela River. Fairmont is actually the port city in America that is furthest from the ocean via an inland waterway (2,085 miles).

The Monongahela flows through Fairmont north to Pittsburgh, Pennsylvania, to the point where that river confluences with the Allegheny River to form the Ohio River that then flows west. The Pittsburgh Pirates once played baseball at Three Rivers Stadium, located near that point.

The Monongahela River divides Fairmont into East Side and West Side. In the later part of the 19th century railroad tracks were laid on both the East Side and the West Side of the River. Walter Coleman Murphy found work in both good times and bad by working for the Monongahela Railroad on one side and the Baltimore and Ohio (B&O) Railroad on the other. Because working for two competing railroads was frowned upon, he was known on one side of the Monongahela as Walter Murphy and on the other side as Coleman Murphy.

His steady work on the railroads was largely a consequence of a booming coal mining business. Between 1890 and 1930 Fairmont was known as the 'Coal City'. Fairmont became the transportation hub and financial center for northern West Virginia's coal fields. In the early part of the 20th century Fairmont was crowded with coal Barons. It was home to more millionaires than anywhere else in the country.

Grandpap was a railroad man but certainly not a railroad Baron. He worked as both a flagman and a conductor of the train. When the train was underway, he rode in the caboose. The caboose was the last car on the train and was like a home on wheels for the crew. It had bunks for sleeping, a small kitchen to prepare and eat meals, and served as an office for the conductor. A 'waybill' followed every freight car from its origin to its destination. The conductor kept the paperwork in the caboose. The caboose was painted red and had a 'cupola' on top that served as an elevated room from which the conductor could observe the entire length of the train ahead.

Grandpap traveled far and wide as a railroad man. Early in his career he worked a line known as the 'Sheepskin Trail'. It was a B&O line that was finished in the 1890's to connect Fairmont with Uniontown, Pennsylvania to the north. It ran first   through

Morgantown, West Virginia where West Virginia University had been founded in 1867, then through Fairchance, Pennsylvania and ended in Uniontown. The story behind the name derived from the fact that the rail line ran through sheep country. When the sheep heard the train whistle, they would scatter, resulting in great consternation to the shepherds. They would yell at the train 'You dang Sheepskinners'! The run was 55 miles long between Fairmont and Uniontown. The town of Fairchance was about 5 miles south of Uniontown, and was the last stop before reaching that final destination. The rural legend was that if you made it to that stop by 4pm you had a 'fair chance' to make it to Uniontown by sundown. The 'Sheepskin Trail' was Grandpap's best route as far as I am concerned. Fairchance is where Grandma lived and that is where they met and fell in love.

When Grace Murphy moved from the family farm near Fairchance to 620 Maryland Avenue in Fairmont her life was changed dramatically. Her home now had electric lights, running water, indoor plumbing & toilet, central coal heat, and a telephone. Her kitchen had an ice box refrigerator and a gas stove and oven. Three separate bedrooms allowed the children and parents to each have their own room.

The world of Grandma Murphy's first two decades of life on Earth had experienced dramatic change. She was thirteen on December 17, 1903 when Wilbur and Orville Wright made their historic first powered airplane flights at Kitty Hawk, North Carolina. The first flight covered a distance of 120 feet and lasted 12 seconds. By their fourth flight the airplane soared for 59 seconds spanning a distance of 852 feet. When she was 18, Henry Ford's newly-invented assembly line mass-produced the first Model T automobile.

During the second, third and fourth decades of the 20th century life in Fairmont had changed dramatically. Schools were still segregated but all children were entitled to a free public education. Schools that the Murphy children attended would be a far cry from a one-room schoolhouse. Telephone service was widely available but limited. You could not call long distances and your phone would be a party line sharing service with up to 10 other families who could listen in on your phone calls. It probably provided for a lot of in-home entertainment.

Those three decades of the 20th century brought even more dramatic changes for the Murphy family and for our country.

The Murphy children were born during World War I, known at the time simply as the 'Great War'. The war had started in 1914 and lasted until an armistice was signed in 1918. America did not enter the war until 1917. Grandpap Murphy was 34 years old at that time, too old to be drafted and obliged to care for his wife and very young children. He did not go to war. But his work as a railroad man would serve the war effort. And he had to be away from home a lot.

During World War I the Wright Brothers' new airplane invention had developed into an incredible fighting machine. Biplanes entered into 'dog fights' using newly-invented machine guns. Henry Ford's mass assembly lines were converted to produce tanks instead of automobiles. And the instruments of war now included the use of poisonous gasses spewing horror into battlefield trenches. The year the war ended in 1918 also brought the Spanish Flu to America. That pandemic killed an estimated 50-100 million people worldwide, including 675,000 Americans.

The impending Great War was also the impetus for greatly changing the system of taxation in America. In 1913 the passage of the 16th Amendment to the Constitution gave Congress the specific authority to levy a tax on the incomes of both individuals and corporations. The first individual marginal tax rates established were 1% on the lowest incomes and 7% on the highest. In 1920, the last year of Democrat Woodrow Wilson's presidency, Congress had increased the respective marginal tax rates to 4% and 73%. During the respective terms of the Republican Presidents of the 1920's, Warren Harding, Calvin Coolidge, and Herbert Hoover, the highest income tax rate was reduced to 25%.

Before the Great War American women had no voice in determining the policies that their country should pursue. Soon after the war on August 8, 1920 the 19th Amendment to the Constitution was ratified, giving women the right to vote. The Republican Party candidate in that November 1920 Presidential election was Warren G. Harding. Harding's Republican Party Platform "reaffirm[ed] its unyielding devotion to the Constitution and to the guaranties of civil, political and religious liberties contained therein." An estimated 36% of eligible women turned out to vote for the first time. And they voted overwhelmingly to elect the Republican candidate President of the United States. Harding carried West Virginia by a 12% margin and secured all of the state's 8 electoral votes. Harding's birthplace was the small town of Blooming Grove, Ohio. It is located about 200 miles from Fairmont. He was a very successful product of rural America and stood for those values, the same values that Grandma had grown-up to share. Although Grandma Murphy always maintained that she was a life-long Democrat, I would wager that her first vote was for a Republican.

There were good reasons for describing the decade of the 1920s as 'roaring'. During the 'Roaring Twenties' the American economy grew by 42%, averaging 4.2% growth in Gross National Product per year. The recent war had destroyed a lot of Europe and the United States began to produce about one-half of the world's industrial output. The automobile industry came alive. The first Model T produced on the 1908 Ford assembly line sold for $850 ($21,000 in today's dollars). Further manufacturing and marketing innovations had made that car available for much less by 1925, when it was sold for $260 ($3,800 in today's dollars). And more families could buy on credit. By the end of the decade 26 million automobiles were registered and women began to drive. Grandpap bought a Model T, but Grandma refused to drive.

As employment became steady and inventions came to market, the manufacture and sales of consumer goods skyrocketed. Grandma Murphy now had a home with a wringer washing machine, a vacuum cleaner and a refrigerator with its own freezer. Times were really good.

Another reason the decade was known as the 'Roaring Twenties' was prohibition. On January 16, 1920 the 18th Amendment to the United States Constitution went into effect. In broad terms that Amendment prohibited the sale and possession of intoxicating alcohol throughout the United States. Most people did not understand that the 18th Amendment would prohibit the sale of beer and wine as well as hard whiskey. As a result, much of the general public simply ignored the liquor law and flocked to illegal 'speakeasys' and underground clubs. Women began to wear more revealing skirts and 'flapper' dresses and began to publicly display less sexual inhibition. More booze was consumed during prohibition than before it. And, as the illegal liquor suppliers prospered, organized crime and the American Mafia began. The unintended consequences would prove to be disastrous. The well-meaning intent of the Amendment was to morally improve the nation. Thirteen years of experiment ended with the repeal of the 18th Amendment by the passage of the 21st Amendment in 1933.

In the prosperous decade of the 1920's nearly everyone became an investor and had a stake in the economy. That was possible because stocks could be bought on 'margin' for about 10% of the stock price. The stock brokers would lend the investor the needed 90%. That practice served to create a lot of wealth during a bull market. But when the market turned south and the brokers called in their loans, the investors were unable to repay them. That practice, along with other poor money policies, resulted in the start of a worldwide economic depression. It began with the crash of the New York Stock Exchange on 'Black Thursday', October 24, 1929. The 'Roaring Twenties' came to an abrupt end.

That Thursday marked the beginning of a worldwide Great Depression that would last for more than 10 years. The breadth and depth of the Depression in our country would result in government programs and policies that would change the role of the Federal government in most dramatic ways.   And those changes would be led by a Democrat, President Franklin Delano Roosevelt.

The Republican Herbert Hoover had been elected President in 1928. During his first year in office he was met with 'Black Thursday' and the start of the Depression.   The Hoover administration and the Republican-dominated Congress took little positive action to address a quickly worsening economic condition.   The monetary policies of the Federal Reserve allowed the large banks to fail. The smaller community banks followed suit and many Americans lost their life savings as banks failed. A shrinking money supply drove what started out as a recession into the Great Depression. The Republicans implemented protectionist trade policies that resulted in a collapse of world trade. They offered loans to farms and businesses but otherwise generally let things run their course. And that economic course proceeded to get worse and worse. Hoover and the Republicans tried to keep the federal budget balanced until 1932. By then it was clear to everyone that such 'hands off' policies were simply not working.

Even nature seemed to conspire to make things worse. In the early 1930's the farms of the Great Plains of the Midwest suffered a severe drought. The practices of overcultivation increased output but ruined the productivity of the soil. Farmers lost their farms and sharecroppers and dispossessed 'Okies' from the 'dust bowl' of Oklahoma migrated west to California in droves. John Steinbeck's novel, *The Grapes of Wrath*, paints an accurate portrait.

By the end of 1932 unemployment had skyrocketed to 25%. As more and more people lost their homes they began to move into neighbor's homes as 'boarders'. They were rented a room in the home for a minimal rent and meals (board) were also provided.

Because of Grandpap's railroad work the Murphy family was able to keep their home during the Great Depression. I do not know for certain if they had borders, but I would conjecture that they did. They were always ready to help out a neighbor. I do know that the Nebraskan Grandmother of my wife, Deneise, did. Boarders were more fortunate than others who simply went hungry. Bread lines and soup kitchens were common. Hobos rode the rail lines in box cars and lived in shanty encampments derisively called 'Hoovervilles'.

This perfect storm of disasters resulted in Democrat Franklin Delano Roosevelt being elected President of the United States in November, 1932. He and a Democratic Congress would then shape the course of the nation for the next two decades.

In his inaugural address FDR proclaimed "The only thing we have to fear is fear itself." And most Americans resolved to believe him and trust that his government solutions would make their lives better and bring back the good times.

FDR wasted no time in implementing drastic federal government measures to provide a 'New Deal' for returning the country back to normalcy. In the first 100 days of the Roosevelt administration in 1933, 12 laws were enacted to address the Great Depression. Three of them provided for major economic reform. The National Industrial Recovery Act suspended some antitrust laws, established an eight-hour work day, and guaranteed that workers would have the right to unionize and bargain collectively for better hours and working conditions. By the time that the United States Supreme Court declared that law to be unconstitutional, most industries had already organized.   The Agriculture Adjustment Act paid farmers for not farming in order to boost agricultural prices by ending surpluses.   The Tennessee Valley Authority Act created the TVA and provided for dams to be built along the Tennessee River and thereby provide hydroelectric power for the first time to light-up a great swath of the South and the Midwest.

In addition to legislation, FDR used the power of Executive Order to establish the Civilian Conservation Corps in 1933 to provide a jobs program for the nation's youth.   Men of ages 18-25 were hired to plant trees, fight forest fires and provide flood controls.   By July 1933 over 1,400 work camps located throughout the country employed over 300,000 young men, paying them $30 per month and requiring them to send $25 back home to support their families.   The CCC had provided employment for an estimated 3 million men during its 9-year life that ended in 1942 with America's entry into World War II.

The thrust of the first 'New Deal' programs had been aimed at revitalizing business and agriculture. But by 1935 the unemployment rate still hovered at 20%. So, FDR shifted his attention to the country's labor force for a second 'New Deal'. He issued an Executive Order creating the Works Progress Administration (WPA). That federal agency would provide government employment for 8 million workers during its 9-year lifetime. WPA labor built National Parks, 4,000 new schools, 130 new hospitals, airfields, bridges and dams.

In 1935 Congress passed the Wagner Act and the Social Security Act. The Wagner Act gave further organizing power to labor unions and created the National Labor Relations Board to put a firm federal presence in union and labor matters. The Social Security Act provided government benefits to the elderly, the widowed and the disabled, and established a program for workers' unemployment compensation. In 1937 the passage of the Railroad Retirement Act provided annuities to aged retired employees based on their years of credible railroad earnings and service.

Germany attacked Poland on September 1, 1939. Great Britain and France responded by declaring war on Germany. World War II had begun. The unemployment rate in the United States at that time was still at 17%. There will always be debate as to how much the 'New Deal' programs did to end the Great Depression. We do know that the programs developed by FDR and the Democrat Congress aimed at ending the Great Depression fundamentally changed the way Americans would view the role of the Federal government in the economy and in their lives. And we do know that after the start of World War II America's 'lend-lease' program, to help Great Britain in its war efforts, gave a great boost to our heavy industry. After the Empire of Japan attacked the United States at Pearl Harbor on December 7, 1941, the unemployment rate in this country dropped to 4.7% in 1942, as the nation mobilized for war. By the time the war ended in 1945 unemployment stood at 1.9%. The Great Depression was now a part of history.

The Murphy family of Fairmont, West Virginia had survived both the Great Depression and World War II. Grandma Murphy had been part of and witnessed great changes in her family. My Uncle Jake had served in the Merchant Marines and had returned to West Virginia to start a new life with a wife in Morgantown, a distant 20 miles from 620 Maryland Avenue. My Father and Mother had become the proud parents of my sister Carolyn and my brother Chet, Jr. The family was able to move to Oak Ridge, Tennessee and be with my Father in base housing as he began his service as a Naval Officer working on the Manhattan Project during World War II. When he was reassigned to sea duty Mother and kids moved back to Fairmont to live with her parents while her husband was away. I entered this world in 1945 and lived in the Murphy household until my Father returned home to recommence civilian life as an electrical engineer. I saw my Father for the first time when I was 9 months old.

During her middle years Grandma Murphy had also been a part of and witnessed great changes in America's culture and way of life.

In 1915, as a young Mother, Grandma Murphy witnessed the birth of the motion picture industry in America. That ushered in a dramatic new way of presenting entertainment to the American public along with a powerful mechanism for influencing public opinion. In that year Hollywood produced its first blockbuster full-length, but silent, movie epic accompanied in each movie theater by live piano music to enhance the drama. The movie was '*Birth of a Nation*' staring Lillian Gish. It was an epic story about the American Civil War and Reconstruction, and it served to glorify and revive the Ku Klux Klan in this country. Democrat President Woodrow Wilson arranged for a private screening of the movie in the White House. After viewing it he praised the film and defended the actions of the KKK. Hollywood became an integral part of American life. The first 'talking' motion picture, '*Don Juan*', was released in 1926. In 1928 the first color movie was produced but the images were blurry. Mickey Mouse made his first cartoon motion picture film debut in that same year as '*Steamboat Willie*'. Drive-in movies debuted in New Jersey in 1933. By 1939 Hollywood had perfected the process of making motion pictures with clear sound and vibrant technicolor with the release of '*Gone With the Wind*' and '*The Wizard of Oz*'.

In 1915 home entertainment was pretty much the same with mostly talking and reading. As the Murphy children, Addamae and Jake, grew-up during the next twenty years, they were introduced to card games like canasta and poker and the board game of checkers. Girls would play jump rope and hopscotch and dolls would provide a world of endless imagination. Boys would jump on pogo sticks, shoot marbles, dangle & cradle YoYos, and play sandlot baseball & football. Youth sports had yet to develop into leagues. Professional Football had begun in earnest in the 1920's when legendary athlete Jim Thorpe was elected president of the American Professional Football

Association, the forerunner of the NFL. Professional players wore leather helmets without face guards. Professional Baseball was the most popular sport of the Twenties and Thirties as fans tuned in to listen to the games of superstars like Lou Gehrig and Babe Ruth of the New York Yankees on the newly-available radio.

The first radios available in the United States were crystal sets that required headphones, and you had to buy the parts separately and build the radio yourself. The invention of the vacuum tube allowed radios to have loud speakers so the family could now sit together and listen. Large scale production of inexpensive radio consoles began in the 1920s, and the legendary plays of Lou and Babe could be heard and imagined over the radio. By the early 1930s nearly everyone had a family radio. That allowed FDR to bring the nation together with his 'fireside chats' during the Great Depression and World War II. Radio would serve to provide a struggling people with welcomed imaginary entertainment at home. Grandma Murphy would start to serve dinner late because Lowell Thomas presented the news of the day at 6:00 pm, followed by the antics of Amos and Andy at 6:30. Those radio favorites just couldn't be missed.

After World War I many of the intrepid biplane pilots of the Army Air Force returned home and began 'barnstorming'. They would demonstrate their aeronautical skills by providing airshows at county and state fares, and they would offer airplane rides for as much as $10 for intrepid passengers. During the 'Roaring Twenties' air travel began to be part of American life. In 1925 Congress passed the Air Mail Act that allowed the U.S. Postmaster to contract with private airlines to deliver the mail. In 1926 Charles Lindberg flew the first American Airlines' flight carrying the U.S. mail from Saint Louis to Chicago. The first scheduled air mail service began in 1930 by a company that would later become known as United Airlines. Because contract payments for mail delivery were based on weight, the companies started to add passenger service to the mail routes. Scheduled passenger service shortly followed, and by 1934 United and American Airlines became the major passenger airlines in the country. And, the airline industry was growing despite the Great Depression. Airline passengers numbered 450,000 in 1934 and grew to 1.2 million by 1938.

To my knowledge neither Grandpap nor Grandma Murphy ever flew in an airplane. But they did pilot the development of their two children during the turbulent years of the Roaring Twenties, the Great Depression and World War II.

Family vacations were few and far between. The vacation mode of transportation was by automobile, for Grandpap loved to drive and he spent his working days on the railroad. These road trips would be aimed at fishing or boating or visiting with members of the extended family. Some dirt roads went through barnyards so you had to get permission to drive through. The longest trip ranged as far as Niagara Falls. The first motel in the country was opened in 1936 in State College, Pennsylvania, home of Penn State University where my Father went to college. Before then overnight stays were spent in tents pitched along the roadways or in the homes of welcoming neighbors operating the first B&B's. Daily progress in travel would be about 100 miles, as stops would be required to add water to an overheated radiator after it had sufficient time to cool. And flat tires occurred early and often. A car tire was narrow and thin and had an inner tube that often leaked and required repair. This was done by jacking-up the car, removing the lug nuts and the tire from the wheel, pulling out the inner tube, repairing it with a glued-on patch, placing the inner tube back in the tire, inflating it with a bicycle hand pump, putting the tire back on the wheel, replacing the lug nuts, lowering the car from the jack, and then taking a rest from all that work.

My Mother and my Uncle Jake never went hungry and continued to receive a solid education. Mother graduated from East Fairmont High School in 1933 and her family was fortunate to be able to afford the $25 tuition per semester to attend Fairmont State College, a fully-accredited institution. She joined a sorority and earned a Bachelor of Arts Degree, which allowed her to become a teacher at East Fairmont High in 1937. Soon after, she met my Father, Chester Samuel Conrad, fell in love and married him in 1938, at age 23.

My Father was a proud American citizen and he was of sturdy stock. His great, great, grandfather, John Jacob Conrad, was born in 1796 and was one of 11 brothers who came to the United States from Holland. He settled in western Pennsylvania to begin a family. My Father's great grandfather, George Conrad, was a coal prospector and earned a 10% finder's fee by locating coal deposits for big landowners. One fee provided him with 1,000 acres of hard coal (anthracite) land, which he later lost by not being able to pay the taxes. He was killed in the Civil War fighting for the North. My Father's grandfather, also named John Jacob Conrad, moved the Conrad family from the Pennsylvania community of Freemont, to Morrisdale and then to Nantyglo, Pennsylvania in 1900. That is where my Father's Father, also named George Conrad, met and married Margaret Evans and welcomed my Father into the world in 1908.

My Grandpa Conrad had moved to Fairmont with his family in 1931 to begin work as foreman of Consolidation Coal Company's central shop in the Marion County town of Monongah. In 1907 Monongah was the site of the worst coal mining disaster to date. The lives of 362 men were lost in a huge underground methane explosion that drove Congress to create the Bureau of Mines.

My Grandpa was an innovative and resourceful fellow. His work would help keep the machinery necessary for coal mining at that time running properly. He invented and built the first coal 'skip loader'. That invention greatly reduced the labor necessary to fill the coal cars. Before the 'skip loader' was invented the miners had to fill the coal cars by the back-breaking work of manual shoveling. He signed over his rights to the 'skip loader' invention to Consol. That was likely one of the main reasons that he kept his steady job during the Great Depression and likely one of the reasons that Consol hired my Father after he graduated from Penn State University as an Electrical Engineer in 1931.

In 1945 Grandma Murphy's nuclear family now included a son-in-law and three grandchildren.

Simply as an author's convenience, that year will designate the conclusion of Grace Swaney Murphy's middle years. Now at the age of 55, she has experienced quite an eventful life. Let's turn now to see what comes next in her Later Years.

CHAPTER 4

MURPHY'S LATER YEARS

My Father returned home from military service in February, 1946. The Conrad family soon moved 17 miles south of the Murphy home in Fairmont to establish a home in Bridgeport at 133 Newton Street. My Father regained steady employment with Consol, and my Mother would be busy raising three young kids.

As we grew-up in Bridgeport my Mother and Father taught us the values that would shape us for the rest of our lives. Each of the kids had chores. Each of the kids was forced to take piano lessons in order to gain some culture, although only my Sister would go on to successfully play the piano. Each of the kids joined the Scouts. My Mother provided us with an early education and taught us to read and write. Elementary School started with the First Grade, for there was no preschool or kindergarten. Although we lived in a remote community of 3,000, because of the national fear of nuclear war with the Soviet Union, young children practiced 'duck and cover' beneath their desks at school. We attended Sunday School and the First Methodist Church services each Sunday.

My Father taught my Brother and me the game of baseball. Organized sports had begun in the country and we both started playing Little League Baseball at an early age. Because the local communities were so small there were not enough players to sort kids by age. So, each team would consist of players age 8 through 12. Your game could really improve by playing with older kids. My Brother would pitch and I would catch and we got pretty good at it. Our Father would coach and he even built our team a new baseball field, complete with backstop and bleachers for the parents and families to watch the games.

Each of us kids learned the value of money at an early age and learned how to manage money matters. At age 10, my Brother and I had a paper route after school. Some 60 papers had to be delivered door-to-door, and we were responsible for making money collections from the subscribers. If a customer 'stiffed' us we still had to pay the publisher the full amount due. After I finished the fifth grade, the family moved from Bridgeport into a brand-new house at 1121 Ridgewood Road in Fairmont. That move allowed my Father to be closer to his work in Monongah, and for my Mother to rekindle a working career at East Fairmont High School teaching English and Speech. It also allowed us to be closer to Grandma Murphy. Grandpap had died in 1954. Our home was on Fairmont's West Side and Grandma lived on the East Side of the Monongahela, but that short distance did not separate us much. Each of us kids were privileged to develop a special relationship with our Grandma Murphy.

My Mother and Sister would shop for Grandma and make sure that she had any medicines that she needed. My Brother and I would do some household chores for her. We learned how to cut her grass with a manual push-mower and to trim her hedges the old-fashioned way with pruning clippers. As we grew bigger into our teenage years, she assigned us some heavier duties. We painted her two-story house with two coats of paint that she insisted was necessary. We cleaned the walls throughout her house in the manner that she instructed. That involved scrunching a putty-like substance into a pad, wiping the pad firmly down the wall, then scrunching the pad together again to gain a clean putty surface, and then again wiping the wall. The process was repeated again and again. It took a lot of time and a lot of effort and I have never heard of anyone else using that method. But it was Murphy's way and it resulted in super-clean walls.

Grandma Murphy was a stickler for cleanliness, neatness and economy. Each year after Christmas was over and the ornaments were removed from the Christmas tree, she insisted that the single strands of tinsel that had served as icicles on the tree be individually removed and carefully boxed for storage to be used the following year.

Grandma Murphy had an Irish sense of humor and always had that blarney-stone twinkle in her eye. As we grew closer and closer with her, we started to address her as 'Scratch', because she was always scratching dirt and cleaning. On using that phrase on one occasion she smiled and asked that I stop using it. And, because I had grown to be much larger, she said that using the term Grandma made her feel old. Just drop the Grandma and simply call me Murphy. After that I always did.

After high school each of us kids went on to college. My Sister went to Fairmont State the same as my Mother had. My Brother and I 'went away to school' to enroll at West Virginia University in Morgantown, a distant 20 miles north. It was not a commuter school, for the roads in the winter months were treacherous and driving that distance on the winding roads of West Virginia would require at least an hour's time in good weather. We would return home on holidays and on some weekends. And there were times when we would return just to see Murphy. In my freshman year I missed a Monday final exam for Psychology 101. That weekend Murphy suffered a severe injury when her hand was caught and pulled through the clothes roller wringer mechanism on her washing machine. As I recall that injury required over 60 stiches and was very painful. I thought it was important to not rush off to an exam. My professor allowed me to make-up the exam after I told him what had happened. He said that in his career he had heard a lot of creative excuses for missing an exam, but that was the first time he had ever heard that one.

Our parents deeply believed in higher education and would have gladly financed our way through college as long as we pitched in. Because of the values that we had been taught by my parents and by Murphy, I decided not to just pitch in but to approach the venture as an adult. After I graduated from high school and turned 18, I decided that I was an adult and should act like one. I should pay my own way in life from here on out. But I had a lot of help from my family in order to do that. My Mother would give me more than a few 'gifts' from time to time as mother's are wont to do, and during the summers I did receive free room and board from my parents. And my family helped me secure good paying jobs.

In the summer before my college freshman year my Father got me a job working for Penn Lines Construction Co., a contractor that he used to clear the rights-of-way and build the power lines necessary to bring electricity to Consol's coal mines in the area. Beginning pay was $1.80 an hour and the work day began when the Dodge Power Wagon, that you boarded at the gas station, reached the place in the woods where work had stopped the previous day. The work was brutal, timbering and clearing a 100-foot swath of forest on the hillside. Then the crew would erect the power poles necessary and properly sag the power lines that would bring electricity to the mine. I well remember that I sat down on a log during the 30-minute lunch break of my first working day and wept because I hurt so much. I did show up the next day and the next for work, and eventually it seemed easier. I learned that some people have to work really, really hard doing dangerous things to make a living.

By the next summer I went to work again with the same crew. The company had been renamed Forest Construction Company but the guys were the same. Red was the boss, Gus was the old man on the crew, maybe 40, and the experienced linemen were Stoney and LeRoy. The low man on the totem pole laborer, other than me, was Bob Huff, who swore that the legendary Sam Huff of the Pittsburgh Steelers was his uncle. Years of experience had taught Gus a great deal about life and I learned some fascinating life lessons from him. Gus constantly chewed tobacco and that required him to spit a lot. And I have never forgotten this knowledge that he freely passed on: "It is impossible to spit and fart at the same time." Stoney and LeRoy taught me how to climb a power pole and I got a raise after becoming a lineman 3rd class. I ended that summer working with my Brother on a job that Uncle Jake got for us. Jake was the Superintendent of a coal mine near Morgantown and had contracted with a painting crew from Pittsburgh to sand-blast and spray-paint the 3-mile-long continuous conveyor belt that connected the mine with the distant tipple. The mine was shut down completely for a 'miners' holiday'. Our job had to be completed in two weeks tops before the miners returned to work. So, we worked 12 hours a day for 14 straight days. The work was grueling, carrying bags of sand to feed to the hoppers that the blasters used, and dragging 5-gallon cans of 'red lead' paint up the steep hillsides that housed the conveyor belt. Each of those paint cans must have weighed at least 200 pounds. But at $2.75 an hour the pay was great. We were paid time and a half for four hours overtime each work day, time and a half all day Saturday and double time on Sunday. We became rich.

I honestly do not remember whether it was my Uncle Jake or my Father who got me a job during the next two college summers working in the Loveridge coal mine at Fairview in Marion County. It had to be one or the other for only they would have had the pull to get a college kid a summer job in the mines. The pay was really good and I became a union man, a card-carrying member of United Mine Workers, District 31. I learned a lot about coal mining and dangerous work. And I learned that there was no place in life for racial or ethnic prejudice. During my first few days on the job, resentment against me ran high and I got pushed around a lot in the shower room. I gained a protector in the first Black man that I ever got to really know. His name was Jessie Smith and he was big, really big, and nobody ever messed with Jessie. And Jessie let everybody know that if they messed with the 'college boy' they would have to mess with him. Problem solved.

Those jobs enabled me to fully pay for college without taking part-time work during the school year. That allowed me to join a fraternity and have a great social life as well as a good education during those four years.

After we finished college the Conrad kids went their separate ways. My sister married and moved to up-state New York. My brother moved to settle on the

California side of Lake Tahoe, and I began working life in San Diego. We would never live in West Virginia again and we returned only for brief visits and for funerals. Murphy's funeral was in 1974.

In the 29 years that I had the pleasure of sharing Murphy's life, Fairmont and the nation had again experienced great change. Murphy still lived in the same house in Fairmont on Maryland Avenue. Her life dramatically changed in 1954 when Grandpap Murphy passed away. The home would never be the same again and she made some changes. The coal chute was sealed and the coal furnace was converted to natural gas. Linoleum was installed on top of some of the hardwood floors so that she could keep them cleaner. Her new refrigerator now had a freezer that didn't require defrosting, but she held on to that stupid wringer washing machine. Home air conditioners became popular in the 1950s and became standard for most new homes built by the 1970s. Murphy's home never had an air conditioner because she believed in fresh air and sunshine.

During the 1950s the 'Golden Age of Radio' was slowly replaced by television as the primary mode of home entertainment. The three major radio broadcast networks, ABC, NBC and CBS, added TV programming to home entertainment choices. Milton Berle was a comedian who became a very popular radio personality in the late forties. He made the successful transition to television as he hosted the *Texaco Star Theater* in 1951 and became known as

'Mr. Television'. Other radio stars such as Jack Benny, Bing Crosby, Bob Hope, Groucho Marx and Abbott & Costello also successfully migrated to the new TV format. Others did not. Most programs were not prerecorded, they were performed 'live' and thereby provided for a lot of hilarious 'bloopers'. Television sets were furniture. General Electric and RCA manufactured 21-inch console TVs that were so heavy that most of the family was required to lift them and place them in a prime viewing spot of the living room. TV remote controls had yet to be invented. All the TV sets had a plastic dial that was used to change channels. Most families had to hunt-up a pair of pliers in order to turn the stem of the plastic dial that had long-ago broken. My Father was a professional engineer who devised a much-handier solution. He permanently attached a pair of 'vise grips' to the stem to correct the problem. Network affiliated TV stations signed off each night by playing the National Anthem at 1:00 am and then displayed a 'test pattern' until programming was resumed about 5 hours later. In 1954 NBC began broadcasting 'The Tonight Show'. It aired each weeknight for ninety minutes, beginning at 11:30 pm. Murphy almost never missed that show and became a night owl as the show transitioned from Steve Allen to Jack Paar to Johnny Carson. Early reception of TV signals in the home was done by an antenna. You had to constantly adjust the antenna in order to get less 'snow' in the picture. Cable TV service started in areas of the country that were remote and inaccessible, like the hill country of northern West Virginia. Fairmont got cable TV, and Murphy thereby got clear TV reception in the 1950s. I was living in San Diego, California in the early 1970s when cable television service first became available in that major city. The hill people of Fairmont had access to modern cable TV service for about 20 years before the city folks living on the west coast.

Telephone service had greatly improved. AT&T was still the sole provider of telephone service in Fairmont and remained so throughout Murphy's life. She still had a dial telephone, but her party line had been replaced by private service, and she could make all the long-distance calls that she wanted.

Automotive transportation experienced dynamic growth after World War II. In 1956 President Dwight David Eisenhower signed into law the development of a 41,000 mile "National System of Interstate and Defense Highways." Road trips became more and more popular. Our favorite family car for such trips was a 1959 Desoto with huge fins, a 300 horsepower V-8 engine and a pushbutton transmission. It used a lot of gas but gas was inexpensive. In the 1950s and 1960s the family vacations were mainly sight-seeing car trips, one to New York City and one to Washington, DC. Two car trips went outside the country for viewing Niagara Falls and fishing at a lake in Ontario, Canada. Murphy stayed home. She didn't like long car trips. Murphy never flew in an airplane and my first flight was during college in 1966. By the late 1950s commercial airlines had begun jet service using Douglas DC-8s and

Boeing 707s. Seats were assigned in both smoking and non-smoking areas. Smoking was very popular at the time, and cigarette commercials still featured physicians extolling the benefits and smooth taste provided by their preferred brand. Rocket travel to outer space developed during Murphy's Later Years and in 1969 Astronaut Neil Armstrong took "One small step for man, one giant leap for mankind" as he descended from his spacecraft onto the surface of the moon.

During her later years Murphy's devotion to the Democratic Party grew even stronger. Democrat President Kennedy's vision and leadership had literally put a man on the moon. And the Democratic leadership of President Lyndon Baines Johnson enacted the Civil Rights Act in 1964 and the Voting Rights Act in 1965. Great strides were made toward guaranteeing civil rights and voting rights for minorities. And Democrat LBJ provided his vision for 'The Great Society' as he declared 'War on Poverty' and created the social programs he felt necessary to win the war. The Economic Opportunity Act of 1964 provided a Head Start Program to help very young children of low-income families. And he created the Office of Economic Opportunity to administer Job Corps, Head Start, VISTA, and community development block grants to provide a hand at the local level. Medicare and Medicaid were sponsored by Democrats and became law in 1965. Murphy believed in helping the less fortunate by giving them a 'hand up and not a hand out', and she strongly felt that these programs would do just that.

It is true that funding for Social Security, Medicare and Medicaid increased dramatically and the poverty rate dropped during the tenure of the Republican President who succeeded LBJ. Richard Milhous Nixon created the Occupational Safety and Health Administration (OSHA) to protect the American worker. Further Nixonian legislation included the National Environmental Policy Act of 1969 and the Clean Air Act of 1970. And in that same year, by Executive Order, he created the Environmental Protection Agency (EPA). Murphy would have favored all those things and may have started to lean a little toward Republicans. But in her final years she followed the unfolding of 'Watergate', the political election scandal that resulted in Republican President Nixon being the first President of the United States to resign in disgrace in our nation's history. It is easy to see why Murphy would be a staunch Democrat through her dying day.

In 1903 the Wright Brothers introduced America to the world of human aviation by successfully soaring a powered airplane for a distance of 852 feet in 59 seconds. Murphy vicariously witnessed that fantastic accomplishment at age 13. At age 79 she actually witnessed on her television set Astronaut Neil Armstrong stepping onto the surface of the moon. Five years later Murphy passed away. Two months before that Murphy asked me to make a promise that I would swear to never break. What was that promise and why has it been so significant in my life?

CHAPTER 5

MURPHY'S PROMISE

A promise usually has two parts. The first part is the request from the person wanting the promise (that would be Murphy). The second part is the pledge from the person agreeing to the promise (that would be me).

Murphy's promise was that I would pledge to always be a registered Democrat. Murphy wanted me to make that pledge and I did so. Not once, but twice.

The first time that Murphy asked me to make that pledge was in 1966 when I turned 21 years old and was first eligible to vote. Before I registered to vote she asked me to promise that I would always be a registered Democrat. Murphy always voted and she voted a straight party line. That was made easy at the time in West Virginia. All you had to do was place one X under either the Republican elephant's trunk on the ballot or under the tail of the Democrat donkey. Grace Murphy always put an X under the donkey's tail.

To me, at that time, the promise was no big deal. Everyone in my family had always been a registered Democrat. And I had a very favorable view of the Democratic Party, mainly due to John Fitzgerald Kennedy.

In the spring of 1960, I joined the crowd assembled outside of the Palace Restaurant in downtown Fairmont to witness a most remarkable event. A candidate for President of the United States of America was actually visiting Fairmont, West Virginia. The legendary JFK was actually eating lunch in the restaurant where everybody in Fairmont had eaten at one time or another. After his lunch he spoke to the crowd outside. JFK inspired awe in this teenager and his challenge rang true. "Ask not what your country can do for you. Ask what you can do for your country."

JFK's challenge rang true for it was in keeping with what had been instilled in me by my family. JFK was a Democrat. All of my family were Democrats. Democrats believe in patriotism and service to your country.

Service to country ran deep in my family. My Great, Great Grandfather George Conrad was killed in the Civil War fighting for the Union to rid the country of slavery. My Grandpap Murphy served in the Army before WWI. My Father served as a Naval Officer in WWII. My Uncle Jake had also served his country in the Merchant Marines.

When JFK fell to an assassin's bullet in 1963, I was a freshman in college. That was a devastating blow to our nation and to me personally. To me JFK represented the ideal leader for our country. He stared down the Soviet Union as he demanded the removal of nuclear missiles from Cuba. He saved the world from war by his courage and resolve. And his entire life bore testament to his personal courage and patriotism through his heroic service as a Naval Officer in the Pacific during World War II. And JFK was always a Democrat.

Immediately following my college graduation, I enlisted in the Navy, attended Officer Candidate School and was commissioned a Naval Officer. The same as my Father and the same as JFK.

The second time that Murphy asked me to pledge always to be a registered Democrat was in 1974. That was the year that I finished night-school and graduated from the University of San Diego School of Law. And that was the year that Grace Murphy passed away.

My last visit with Murphy was two months before her death. She was at that time very frail and found words to be hard. She was figuratively on her deathbed. But even at that time she was certain and adamant in her political conviction. She asked me to reconfirm the promise that I would pledge to always be a Democrat and I did so.

That reconfirmation was more difficult because of my life experience during the years intervening between the first promise and the second iteration.

In December, 1973 I joined the staff of Mayor Pete Wilson in San Diego, California. When Pete invited me to join his staff I eagerly accepted. But not before I disclosed to him that I was a registered Democrat. He asked me why? And I told him of Murphy's promise and that I simply could not break that promise. I well remember Pete's smile as he shook my hand and welcomed me aboard. We never discussed the matter again. Pete was always a Republican and always a true gentleman.

The years that I worked for Mayor Pete greatly changed my views of the Republican Party. Pete had served his country as a Marine Corps Officer. He embodied hard work, thoughtfulness and integrity. I remember well one certain day when just the two of us worked together on a most-thorny project until we finished it at 3 o'clock in the morning. Before we began in the late afternoon, he asked me if I minded working late. And by the time we had concluded he looked a lot less tired than I felt and he was certainly better groomed. He had never loosened his tie.

In December, 1977 I left Pete's staff to join a private law firm. My years in his office, where I was the sole Democrat, were enjoyable and enlightening. All those Republicans were very welcoming. Everyone dealing with the Mayor's Office was treated with dignity and respect. I never observed any discrimination. The stereotype of a Republican that my West Virginia roots had instilled in me was that of a discriminatory bigot who cares for the rich and looks down on the working man. What my life experience had shown me was that the stereotype was simply not true.

Apparently, most of the folks in California at that time did not believe in that Republican stereotype either. Pete Wilson was reelected Mayor of San Diego, went on to serve as a United States Senator, and was twice elected Governor of the State of California.

Most unfortunately stereotypes have a way of perpetuating themselves and spreading. That seems to be especially true for political stereotypes. And most especially true if your political opponent is very skilled in developing uniform talking points that are aimed with precision to embed negative images in the nation's consciousness.

The leaders of the Democratic Party are in lock-step with the talking points that Republicans are racists, misogynists, haters, and all-around evil bigots. And they are also in lock-step with the talking points that Republicans care only for their rich friends and care nothing for the workers, the poor and the oppressed.

How could any decent person become a Republican?

In the next few chapters I will attempt to determine the best answer to a most significant question in my life. If Murphy were alive today would she still be adamant in her Democrat political allegiance? Would she still want me to keep Murphy's Promise?

CHAPTER 6

MURPHY'S VIEWS ON POLITICS

I have had the privilege to be influenced by many strong and independent women in my life. The two that were the most influential were my Mother and Grandma Murphy. They were Irish Americans through and through and they did not suffer fools. They believed that our elected government representatives should derive the best solutions to the thorny problems of society by the free exchange of opinions and evidence in civil debate. To them that represented *politics*. Voters should decide which candidates should be elected, and by extension which political party should hold the majority of representatives, in order to determine two things: governmental policies and programs; and the effectiveness of those policies and programs.

Murphy's devotion to the Democratic Party was founded upon and grew through the policies and programs instituted during the Great Depression of the 1930's. The CCC and WPA jobs programs provided government employment to millions of American citizens during a time of national crisis. The working man was given a leg-up by the National Recovery Act that provided for an 8-hour workday and the right to join a union. Security in old age was provided by the Social

Security and Railroad Retirement Acts. All these things were done by the leadership of a President and a majority of Congress who were solidly Democrat. Her devotion further grew during the 1960's when Democrat President Lyndon Baines Johnson spearheaded the Civil Rights Act of 1964 and the Voting Rights Act of 1965, and established the government programs to create the Great Society. And in her final years she followed the unfolding of Watergate, the political election scandal that only ended when Republican President Richard Milhous Nixon was forced to resign the Presidency in 1974 in shame, for the first time in our nation's history. It is easy to see why she would want me to make Murphy's Promise. She was a patriotic American who supported a government that looked out for hard-working Americans and for equality and opportunity for all. She deeply believed that the Democratic Party was the party that would always do that. It was very important to her that Democrats should always retain control of the policies and programs that would provide for these things, even after she was no longer on this Earth. She wanted me to swear that I would always be a registered Democrat, and I did so.

What Murphy could not possibly foresee were the unintended consequences of the Great Society Programs that became institutions in our country. In the name of social justice and ending poverty, urban ghettos were created in America's great cities, including the nation's largest, Chicago, New York City, and Los Angeles. Most of our great cities have been under solid Democrat control for the past fifty years. Poverty and homelessness have only increased during that half century and the federal housing projects created for the poor have become slums. Minority families have been decimated by these policies and now only 1 in 5 minority children have a father in the home to teach them the values needed for a successful life. The Democrat policy approach is simply to throw more taxpayer money into supporting failed policies. Democrats stress that education of underprivileged children must be provided only by traditional schools because the Teachers Union supports Democrats and opposes Charter Schools that have been demonstrated to better-help these students. It is unconscionable that after 50 years of Democrat leadership in these communities the kids are simply not getting properly educated. The cities that have the worst public education record have been run by Democrats for decades. As a nation our high school graduation rate has increased to 88%. But that is far from the experience of poor and minority students. In New York City the graduation rate is a mediocre 71%, but for Black and Hispanic males the rate is a dismal 37%. Other major cities that have been run by Democrats for decades include what ABC News reports as the 5 worst cities for urban youth: Cleveland, Baltimore, Atlanta, Detroit and Chicago. The poor graduation rates in those cities ranges from 34% in Cleveland to 56% in Chicago. Graduating high school goes a long way toward qualifying to get a good job. Our kids deserve a better approach than simply throwing more money into failed programs. Another policy approach is desperately needed to address the systemic problems faced by minority Americans today.

Most of the poor and disadvantaged American citizens are Hispanics and Blacks. The Democrat approach to the very real problems of poverty and social stagnation for the poor and disadvantaged in our society is to not provide the opportunities required to gain a substantial income through better education and preparation for better employment. Rather, the approach is to simply provide the poor and disadvantaged with government funding that will allow the citizens of this country who are poor and disadvantaged to have a subsistence existence without working. By doing so the Democrats expect to be rewarded for their largess by counting on the votes of the poor and disadvantaged. In large measure that ploy has been very successful. The last President to obtain a majority of minority votes in this country was Herbert Hoover in 1928. In the 2016 election Republican Donald Trump secured only 29% of the Hispanic vote and a mere 8% of the Black vote.

Murphy would have liked Trump's straight talk and refusal to engage in political correctness. She would have liked the programs that he spearheaded to actually help the poor and disadvantaged Americans who need help the most. The Republican approach is to attempt to provide a good job for every American who is able to work. That will not only provide a middle-class income, it will bolster individual pride and personal liberty. After three years in office the

Republican approach has spearheaded Prison Reform and Opportunity Zones through legislation and an Apprenticeship Program by Executive Order. The Apprenticeship Program is designed to provide a path to a good job with a good future through meaningful work. Opportunity Zones are designed to provide for private investments to revitalize the poorest neighborhoods in our country by building infrastructure and developing blighted properties. The First Step Act for Prison Reform: expands prison rehabilitation programs; reduces mandatory prison sentences; and cuts 53,000 years off of existing prison sentences. These are Republican approaches to address real problems with real solutions. Not just putting more money into failed policies. The Republican approach is to provide a social safety net for the poor and disadvantaged while at the same time increasing prosperity for everyone by supporting free markets through capitalism. The Democrat approach of advancing 'social justice' by democratic socialism will simply result in bringing all of society to the lowest common denominator. That is not the American way. Murphy would support the Republican approach.

Murphy would have been appalled at many of the things that Trump crudely says and she would have intensely disliked the derisive nicknames whereby he characterizes opponents. So, in deciding whether to support Trump she would have to make a choice. What is more important: the crude things that he says; or, the policies and programs that he both supports and actually accomplishes?

In trying to answer that question I am helped by two adages that guided Murphy's actions throughout her life. The first guiding adage is: 'The road to hell is paved with good intentions'. The policies and programs that the Democrats spearheaded in the 1960s were clearly intended to help the poor and disadvantaged American citizens. The results of those policies and programs after half a century and the investment of literally trillions of taxpayer dollars in them, clearly show that they have not worked. In 1964, before the War on Poverty began, 36 million Americans lived in poverty. In 2018, 38 million Americans live in poverty. And the poor and disadvantaged Americans living in slums in major American cities experience not only poverty but a poor education for their children and the virtual disappearance of two-parent households. The second guiding adage is: 'Actions speak louder than words.' From January, 2009 until January, 2017 Democrat Barack Obama was President of the United States. He was a gifted orator and his words were inspirational. His actions were not very impressive. During his tenure the American economy remained stagnant and he exhibited little restraint in using Executive Orders to accomplish things that should only be done through laws passed by Congress. His words spoke much larger than his legitimate actions. But he still provides the most dynamic leadership of the Democratic Party.

By tradition in this country, ex-Presidents do not insert themselves into the campaigns of future Presidential candidates. The candidates themselves should express their own views and conduct their own campaigns. On May 21, 2020, I received a letter from President Barack Obama. He asks that I contribute money to the DNC's Democratic Unity Fund. He explains that:

"The Democratic Unity Fund is a promise – a promise that whoever earns our nomination will have a strong, unified, and well-prepared DNC ready to lift them to victory from the moment the general election starts. People like you have always fueled my faith in the future, and I know I can count on you to help the DNC strengthen critical programs like Organizing Corps 2020. This is an unprecedented investment in the next generation of Democratic leaders – a massive commitment to train college students as field organizers in key battleground states this year. Organizing Corps 2020 is rooted in the spirit that drove both of my campaigns – the belief that one voice can change the mood of a room, which in turn can change the mood of the neighborhood, and then a city, and then a country. And then, you change the world. That is the optimism – and the commitment to hard work on the ground that has always led Democrats to victory."

President Obama tells me that I must support *whoever earns our nomination*. The merits of the individual selected by the Party are not important. It is simply assumed that all registered Democrats must vote the straight party line.

Murphy and my Mother were school teachers. They believed in teaching students the basics of education so that they would become lifelong learners for themselves. They taught facts, not propaganda. Today our children are being indoctrinated with progressive ideology debasing our history, and many of their teachers, from preschool through high school graduation, advocate social change in the classroom. This has happened before in recent history in Europe when Germany's youth were indoctrinated with the message of social change needed in the 1930s – national socialism. Today in our country when students enter our colleges and universities for higher education, they are taught by liberal professors that America is an evil society based on racism and hate and must be changed through a progressive agenda. Anyone with views contrary to the progressive agenda is demonized and unwelcome. College administrators classify such contrarian views as 'hurtful' and students must be protected from them. Our First Amendment guarantee of freedom of speech is today restricted on the college campus to 'free speech zones.'

The traditional approach to higher education in college has been to have the 'academic freedom' for students and professors to debate ideas by exchanging opposing views. Every issue has two sides and you can learn a lot simply through the exercise of debate. My Mother taught debate and she taught it well.

In the late 1960s and early 1970s the ratio of progressive professors to conservative professors on our college campuses was about 3 to 2: Three progressives to two conservatives. That made for a healthy debate. By 2020 the ratio for incoming professors has become about 50 progressives to 1 conservative. And the one conservative is never invited to debate. The conservative voice is simply shouted down and the conservative professor becomes reviled on college campus.

In this upside-down *Alice in Wonderland* world of academia today, the term 'academic freedom' is now used to protect students from the evils of opposing views in objective debate. Students are to be exposed only to the propaganda taught by progressive professors. Instead of being taught to think for themselves, they are taught that they must simply follow the progressive party line. Their job is not to think. Their job is to spread the message of Progressive Democrats.

Our English dictionary provides us with a word passed down from the ancient Greeks that describes loyal student followers who execute the orders of the Progressive agenda unquestionably or unscrupulously – Myrmidons.

President Obama's call for a massive commitment to train college students as Myrmidon field organizers to spread the message of the needed change to the country and the world is all the evidence needed to show just how frightening this radical approach is.

What would Murphy have done if she received that letter? Would she want to support a Democratic Party that wants to make a massive commitment to train college students as field organizers? Would she want to change the country and then change the world?

Murphy was a proud American citizen. She did not want to change America and change the world. She wanted to work within the framework of this country to improve life for all citizens using the founding principles of our Declaration of Independence and our Constitution. We citizens are all created equal and endowed with unalienable rights of life, liberty and the pursuit of happiness. Those rights come from God, not the government. Government is established by the People to ensure that those rights are not abridged. Government is not established in order to tell us how we should live in America. How we live is up to us as proud American citizens who are part of an American community. It is a community of liberty and freedom. When government encroaches into our basic freedoms it has gone too far and must be curbed. That is done not by force but by the ballot box. The massive intrusion into our individual liberty and freedom that is advocated by the modern Democratic Party is anathema to this country's founding principles. The stated goals of today's Democratic Party agenda are to fundamentally change America and then to change the world. Murphy would never have supported such an agenda.

What the Democratic Party has done to politics in the last half century would have disgusted Murphy. And it has never been worse than now. Democrats refuse to engage in debate on political issues facing our nation, because they know the merits of their positions cannot possibly be supported by the vast majority of Americans in this country. Instead, they engage in character assassination, the lowest form of political argument. Most regrettably, the mainstream media of this country have abandoned any attempt to inform the American people about political issues. Instead, they assist in championing the smear agenda of the Democrats as abettors of a partisan effort to simply regain full control of our government by the Democratic Party. That would be disastrous for our nation because the actual political agenda of the Democratic Party leadership has become identified as the 'goals' of the 'Green New Deal'. And that those goals should be accomplished through a 10-year national mobilization. House Resolution 109 includes these specific provisions that would permanently convert our republican form of government into a socialist state and proclaims that:

> "It is the duty of the Federal Government to create a Green New Deal. To achieve the Green New Deal goals and mobilization, a Green New Deal will require the following goals and projects:

> (C) providing resources, training, and high-quality education, including higher

education, to all people of the United States, with a focus on frontline and vulnerable communities, so that all people of the United States may be full and equal participants in the Green New Deal mobilization.

(H) guaranteeing a job with a family-sustainable wage, adequate family and medical leave, paid vacations, and retirement security to all people of the United States;

(O) providing all people of the United States with:

- high-quality health care;
- affordable, safe, and adequate housing;
- economic security; and
- clean air, healthy and affordable food, and access to nature."

It is important to note that the Federal Government must provide all of these things not just to American citizens. 'All people of the United States' is an intentionally-crafted term. It clearly means that all these things are to be provided to anyone living in our country, without regard to legal status.

It is also more than just interesting to note that under Joseph Stalin's 1936 Constitution all citizens of the Soviet Union were guaranteed:

- a job with a sustainable wage;

- free medical service for all;
- paid vacations and retirement security for all;
- free college and university education.

Such a utopian society can only be attained by giving dictatorial powers to the government elite, and that is exactly what happened in Russia. The citizens were also guaranteed that women would have equal rights and women would receive free prematernity and maternity leave with full pay; and that there would be no racial discrimination in all spheres of economic, state, cultural, social, and political life. Freedom of speech, press, assembly and religion were also guaranteed to the Russian people. All of this would be achieved through Stalin's 5-year plans and autocratic power. History has shown the actual results of this utopian society where millions of Soviet citizens were not only deprived of fundamental freedoms but were intentionally starved to death or murdered. That was accomplished by the amassing of central power in a totalitarian state. In her lifetime Murphy witnessed the horrors of socialist democracy that the Soviets called Communism. Murphy would never have supported such a system that is anathema to everything American.

HR 109 was cosponsored by 99 Democrat members of the House of Representatives, including Jerry Nadler and Adam Schiff, the powerful Chairmen of the House Committees appointed by Speaker Nancy Pelosi to lead the movement to Impeach Donald Trump. The Green New Deal was cosponsored in the United States

Senate by 9 Democrat Senators, including 7 Senators seeking the Presidency in the 2020 election.

The Green New Deal does not represent some fringe element of the Democratic Party. It represents the thinking of mainstream elected Democrat leaders today. They actually want to transform the United States of America into a socialist state. Indeed, Joe Biden, the presumptive nominee of the Democratic Party for the 2020 Presidential election, made his position clear during the 4th Democrat debate on October 19, 2019 when he advocated his support for the Green New Deal.

The Green New Deal, contained in HR 109, was not brought to a vote by the Speaker of the House of Representatives. The Speaker would not bring the resolution to a vote so that elected Democrat officials would never have to be put on record for their vote. The political correctness of elected Democrat officials apparently requires astute artful-dodging of the issues.

And, when the Green New Deal was put to a vote in the Senate, the Democrats accused the Republican Leader in the Senate of 'playing politics' by seeking a vote on the matter. Somehow in the upside-down *Alice in Wonderland* world of Democrats today, voting on an issue of importance to let the People know where you stand is deemed to be 'playing politics'. Even the nine Democrat Senators who sponsored the bill joined 34 other Democrat Senators in not taking a stand. They simply voted 'Present' instead of Yes or No. Only two

Democrats and **all Republican Senators opposed the Green New Deal with a No vote.**

Playing politics is not the American way. The Democrats have made an art form of that practice, which is the subject of the next chapter.

CHAPTER 7

MURPHY'S VIEWS ON PLAYING POLITICS

Murphy abhorred politicians who *'played politics'*. That is a term that has been in use, ever since 1853 when Republican abolitionist Wendell Phillips declared: "We do not *play politics*; anti-slavery is no half-jest to us."

In 1871 Lewis Carroll published a sequel to his brilliant political satire of British life of the times titled *Alice in Wonderland*. In *Through the Looking Glass* Alice enters a world turned upside down where black is white and dark is light. Running helps you stay put. Walking away from something brings it closer. Everything is reversed in this world, including logic. The modern Democratic Party has been quite successful in creating such a wonderland here in America in 2020 by *playing politics*.

The elected leaders of the Democratic Party today have turned legitimate politics upside down by refusing to engage in the free exchange of ideas and evidence in civil debate. Instead, with no sense of decency, they hatefully engage in character assassination of Republicans. The tactic is simple. And, it has been highly effective. Destroy your opponent's character and make your opponent the bad guy. Characterize your opponent as an evil person simply not worthy of living, let alone being elected to office.

Two months before the Presidential election of 2016, the Democratic Party candidate for President of the United States, Hillary Clinton, was not content with slandering just her opponent with spurious and unfounded character attacks. She went on to place half of the supporters of her opponent, Republican Donald Trump, into a **'basket of deplorables'** as she described them as **racist, sexist, homophobic, xenophobic** and **Islamophobic.** This is what those terms of character assassination actually mean:

- A racist is someone who believes that their race is superior to another race and that our political system should be founded on such belief.
- A sexist is someone who believes in discrimination against women.
- A homophobe is someone who has an irrational fear of, aversion to, or who believes in discrimination against homosexuals.
- A xenophobe is someone who unduly fears foreigners.
- An Islamophobe is someone who has an irrational fear of, aversion to, or who believes in discrimination against Muslims.

None of those outrageous charges are supported by facts or evidence. And no facts or evidence in support of those outrageous character attacks are ever offered. They are simply repeated as if they are common knowledge. Those charges are the furthest thing from the truth. But a compliant anti-Trump media simply reports those outrageous charges again and again as if they are facts.

When Hillary Clinton leveled her outrageous charges against one-half of the Trump supporters, she was referring to the one-half of his supporters that were men. Her outrageous charges could not apply to women Trump supporters. It would certainly be illogical to declare that women would believe in discrimination against women. But logic be damned.

Now, in the 2020 election year, Hillary Clinton further continues to accuse Trump of negligence, corruption, racism and malevolence evidenced by malicious ill will, spite and hatred. The elected leadership of the Democratic Party have completely abandoned logic and simply announce that anyone who would support Republican Donald Trump must be a racist, sexist, homophobic, xenophobic, Islamophobic bigot. If you are a Republican you simply must be the worst all-around hater that can ever be imagined. Only a despicable person would remain a Republican. That is the core Democrat message of politics today. Issues need not be decided by the free exchange of ideas and evidence in civil debate. Issues should be decided by whether someone is a good person or an evil person, and which person do you identify with, good or evil?

The presumptive Democratic Party candidate for President of the United States in the 2020 election is Joe Biden. On June 4, 2020, 151 days before that election, Joe Biden accused Donald Trump of dividing the nation, adding that as president he would bring the people together. In describing how he would bring the people together he added this specific message:

> "There are probably anywhere from **10 to 15 percent of the people out there that are just not very good people**, but that's not who we are. The vast majority of the people are decent, and we have to appeal to that and we have to unite people – bring them together."

Let's examine Joe Biden's message of unity in a little more detail. He is, after all, the candidate that Democrats support to become the next President. On June 4, 2020 the population of the United States is 330 million people. Mr. Biden believes that between 10% and 15% of the people are **just not very good people.** So, apparently, he is going to unite the country by casting aside between 33 million (10%) and 49.5 million (15%) of the people by uniting the rest of the people in the country who he apparently feels are very good people. Since that is how he feels, he has a duty to tell us exactly who the **just not very good people** are. In the name of national unity, casting aside and branding as **just not very good people** is the path forward offered by the Democrats. Those outcasts comprise far more Americans than the 27 million people that make up the combined population of our 10 largest cities: New York City; Los Angeles; Chicago; Houston; Phoenix; Philadelphia; San Antonio; San Diego; Dallas; and San Jose.

The Democrats have become the masters of political division and very adept at ignoring the merits of their political positions while destroying the character of their opponents. And that is abhorrent to Murphy's beliefs and views.

Another aspect of playing politics that the Democrats now engage in almost exclusively is called 'identity politics'. Identity politics results from the grouping of different people in society into specific sects based on things over which they have absolutely no control. White voters. Black voters. Hispanic voters. Asian voters. Male voters. Female voters. Gay voters. Lesbian voters. Transsexual voters. The basic idea is that you must view all issues facing American society today not as a free and proud American. Instead you should vote in lockstep with the other members of the cast into which you have been assigned by birth. Casts must be consumed with grievances, real or perceived, against their casts. That is the Democrat path to achieving social justice. That cast system is simply a ridiculous approach toward achieving social justice in America. Our political system can only work through cooperation and compromise. Regardless of our skin color, our sex or our sexual preference, we are at core all American citizens. We are blessed by God to live in this free nation as free individuals who are most capable of recognizing individual differences and working together to resolve our social problems. Pitting sect against sect is for losers. And it is against all of the founding principles that have made this country the envy of the world. Murphy would shun such identity politics.

In the 1960s, Democrat John Fitzgerald Kennedy challenged Americans: "Ask not what your country can do for you. Ask what you can do for your country."

In the upside-down *Alice in Wonderland* world of the 2020s, Progressive Democrats challenge Americans: "Ask not what you can do for your identity. Ask what your identity can do for you." Both JFK and Murphy would find that to be very sad and against the core beliefs of this great nation.

CHAPTER 8

MURPHY'S VIEWS ON THE ROLE OF GOVERNMENT

My Grandma Murphy and my Mother taught me the role of government. They did not view the matter as complicated or requiring great intellectual sophistication to understand. It was a simple matter. They believed that the role of government is to carry out the will of the People. Carrying out the will of the People would be accomplished by providing equal opportunity and equal justice for all in the manner described in our Constitution. This country was founded on the principles of individual freedom and liberty, and limited government. A famous liberal writer of the 19th century, Henry David Thoreau, in his *Essay on Civil Disobedience*, adopted this adage: "That government is best which governs least." Liberal Democrats then, and Republican conservatives today, adhere to that belief. Government is a necessity for ensuring that the common needs of the community are met while ensuring that individual rights and freedom and liberty are retained to the greatest extent possible. A common need of the community is to provide necessary assistance to the poor and disadvantaged of society who, through no fault of their own, need a helping hand up. And that will always be a proper role of our government. The will of the People is expressed through the vote of the People. That is the foundation of our democratic republic.

As proud Americans, these two powerful women taught that the business of government must necessarily be conducted by individuals serving as government officials. Officials who are elected to government office, or are appointed to office by those elected officials, have a duty to carry out the People's business in a fair and impartial manner. Both elected and appointed government officials swear allegiance to our Constitution and take an oath to do so. The job of government officials is to serve the interests of the People in accord with the vote of the People. Government officials are thereby honorably called 'public servants' and are expected to proudly perform their public duty.

Today's Democrats do not believe in such limited government. They believe that the role of government must be expanded to include, not just equal opportunity, but equal outcomes for all. Regardless of differences in individual efforts toward pursuing happiness, everyone must be limited in their achievements in order to guarantee an equal share of happiness for all. The powers of the Federal government must be used to rectify all social disadvantages. Only by doing that will 'social justice' be achieved. It thereby becomes the role of government to ensure that, not only citizens, but everyone living in America, is given all of the resources that they need from the Federal government in order to live a happy life. And the Federal government – not the People – will determine what a happy life is. That is the proper role of the Federal government that Democrats now believe is necessary and proper in this country. The proof of that is specified in black and white print in HR 109, the Green New Deal. That bill specifies that "it is the **duty** of the Federal Government today to create a Green New Deal." The goals and projects described in that Congressional bill specify a 10-year plan that will, in essence, provide all things to all people. Read HR 109 and see for yourself. Then read the articles of the 1936 Constitution of the Soviet Union and see for yourself how closely those articles, supported by Joseph Stalin's 5-year plans of Communism, align with the goals and projects specified by the Green New Deal.

The expansion of the Federal government beyond that envisioned by our Constitution in not a new idea. The Green New Deal is simply today's ultimate expression of that idea. The separation of powers between three branches of our government is central to our Constitution. The reason for that separation is simple: Power corrupts and absolute power corrupts absolutely. That was not a cynical belief of the nation's founders. That belief was simply based on the fact that government functions only through human beings and that all human beings have personal biases that can taint their objectivity. Democrat Woodrow Wilson thought that such a belief had become outdated. In order to meet the challenges of the times faced by his administration, he felt that vast discretion must be given to Executive Agency Administrators who are 'experts' in their field, and who are always highly competent, selfless, and objective. He expressed a strong Progressive belief in the creation of what is now called the Administrative State. He sincerely believed that by 1913, as he was sworn into office as the 28th President of the United States, American society had progressed to the point where the administration of government should be handled by 'experts' and that those 'experts' were enlightened and free of personal bias. They could be counted on to always be objective in their administration of government offices and would always be free from political partisanship and discrimination.

Ever since the Progressive Democrat movement began under Woodrow Wilson, the discretion of Federal agency administrators has grown greater, and greater, and greater. The Constitution assigns the power to make Federal law exclusively to the Congress of the United States. The 115th Congress began on January 3, 2017 and ended on January 3, 2019. In those two years Congress enacted 442 Federal laws. During that same two years, Federal government Executive Agency Administrators enacted 6,600 Federal laws. They are called final agency rules. But they are in fact laws that must be followed on penalty of fine or imprisonment. Executive Agency Administrators are not elected and are not answerable to the American People for the laws they enact. Our Constitution provides that only the elected members of

Congress have the power to enact laws. If Congress delegates the powers to 'fill in the blanks' to Executive Agency Administrators, then Congress has an affirmative duty to keep a close eye on the Administrators through Congressional oversight. Such oversight is no longer provided when the Democrats hold a majority of seats in either the House of Representatives or the Senate.

On January 3, 2019 the 116th Congress began their work. The House of Representatives was now under the firm control of the Democratic Party leadership. In their first year the current Congress has enacted 138 laws. The remainder of the time has been spent not in the legitimate oversight role of Federal agencies. Rather, the House Democrat majority and the Senate Democrat minority have been consumed by one simple goal. Remove the sitting President of the United States from office. That subject will be reviewed in Chapter 11.

The year before Woodrow Wilson was elected President in 1912, Wilson was the Governor of New Jersey. In 1911 he signed into New Jersey law a Eugenic Sexual Sterilization Act which provided that criminals or adults considered to be 'feeble-minded' would be sexually sterilized. That was in keeping with the Progressive belief of the times in Eugenics, for that was a new 'science' supported by science 'experts'. Eugenics was supposedly an extension of Charles Darwin's Theory of Evolution. The science 'experts' explained that selective improvement of desirable traits in humans could be controlled by 'better breeding', either by inducing young people to fall in love more intelligently or by controlling the propagation of the mentally incompetent through forced sterilization. Progressive science 'experts' continued to follow the dictates of Eugenics for more than 30 years in this country and, under their influence, state after state adopted forced sterilization laws whereby more than 64,000 people were forcibly sterilized in the United States.   The horrors of the science of Eugenics, sponsored by unbiased 'experts', were abandoned in this country only when Adolf Hitler took the 'science' to an unimaginable place with the Holocaust.

The sophisticated reasoning of Progressive Democrats in Woodrow Wilson's time was reminiscent of the upside-down world that Lewis Carroll presented in *Alice in Wonderland*.   In order to be completely objective and unbiased one had to support the Jim Crow laws and the KKK. And unbiased and completely objective government officials had to step-in to make sure such laws were enforced. Progressives just knew that Federal government agencies would always be totally nonpartisan and unbiased as long as Democrats are in charge.

During the era of Eugenics, science 'experts', also called for bans against interracial marriage. A surge of new state laws banning interracial marriage began. The penalty for interracial marriage included prison terms for up to ten years.

As these science 'experts' were proving that they were totally free from political partisanship or discrimination by carrying out the goals of Eugenics and racial discrimination, the Democrat Wilson administration 'experts' were proving the same thing in the administration of the Federal government. Democrat Woodrow Wilson stood by in support as his Federal Administrative Agencies instituted the policy of racial segregation throughout the Federal civil service. All of that, of course, was done with complete objectivity and non-discrimination by the 'expert' administrative class. Progressive Democrats then and now continue to express absolute confidence in an Administrative State that must be free from the checks and balances required by our Constitution. Progressive Modernity of the 21st century in America simply demands it. That is the modern version of Alice's Wonderland, wherein the world and logic are turned upside-down.

What would Murphy have thought of the Democrat Party's vision of the role of government today? The answer is simple. Murphy would abhor it.

Let's turn now to examine the non-partisan, non-discriminatory, unbiased actions of some of the 'expert' Executive Agency Administrators operating within today's Federal Government. Let's see if they are always free of government corruption.

CHAPTER 9

MURPHY'S VIEWS ON GOVERNMENT CORRUPTION

Watergate

The Watergate scandal began on June17,1972 when five burglars, sent by operatives of the Republican National Committee and the Committee to Reelect the President, broke into the offices of the Democratic National Committee Headquarters, located within the Watergate Hotel of Washington, D.C. They were attempting to plant 'wire-taps' on the office phones and steal other campaign information. Some of the Republican operatives who authorized the break-in were later discovered to be high-ranking executive officials of the Nixon administration. Less than five months later Richard Nixon beat Democrat George McGovern to win reelection to office. The outcome was a landslide – 64% to 36%.

Watergate happened because high-level executive government officials used the power of their public offices to engage in illegal political actions. The outcome of the election clearly evidences that such a scheme was totally unnecessary. But these officials felt that they couldn't take any chances and that they had the right to use the powers of their public offices to engage in illegal acts and to then attempt to conceal those actions by using the power of their official offices to cover-up those crimes. They believed they could get away with it because they controlled the agencies of government that would investigate those actions. That is a clear abuse of governmental power.

Richard Nixon was not a part of authorizing or conducting the actual Watergate burglary. He did not know about it before it happened. In a taped White House conversation between Nixon and H.R. Haldeman, his chief of staff, a furious president asked: "Who was the a**hole who ordered it?" But after he found out about it, Nixon's crime was using the executive powers of government to attempt to cover-up the criminal conduct of the high-ranking government officials in his administration. That is the crime that Nixon committed. The cover-up is the crime. It is called Obstruction of Justice. When it became clear that convincing evidence would soon be forthcoming that he had used his official powers to cover-up the crimes, he knew he had committed the crime of Obstruction of Justice. He then resigned the Presidency in shame, for the first time in our nation's history.

Murphy was incensed by the corruption of government that Nixon and his Republican Executive Officials had perpetrated on the American people. What would she think about the recent actions of Democrat Executive Officials that demonstrate the same arrogance of office that the Nixon Republicans did? Let's first fast forward to the Hillary Clinton email scandal and see. Then we will take a look at two more scandals grouped together under the heading of Russiagate.

Hillarygate

Hillary Clinton was the candidate chosen by the Democratic Party to challenge Republican Donald Trump in the 2016 Presidential election. Her husband, Bill Clinton, had served as President of the United States from 1993 to 2001. After leaving her position as First Lady of the United States for 8 years, she was elected to the United States Senate, representing the State of New York. In 2008 she ran against Democrat Barack Obama to gain her party's nomination as the Democratic Party candidate for President, but Obama won that nomination and the election. President Obama appointed Hillary Clinton to be Secretary of State in 2009 and she served in that capacity until after Obama's successful reelection in 2012. In February 2013 she resigned her position so that she could pursue the Democratic Party nomination for President in 2016.

Since 2005 State Department Rules have forbidden employees from using private email accounts for government business and forbid employees from using 'sensitive but unclassified' information in private emails. Throughout her tenure as Secretary of State, Mrs. Clinton exclusively used her own private email server in conducting official government business as well as her own personal business. The server that she used for her email was physically located in the basement of her home in New York. The server was not secure. It was eventually discovered that many official highly-classified government communications, including 22 that were classified Top Secret, were accessed on that unsecured server. After a three-year State Department investigation into the propriety of using this private email system to conduct government business, the Department cited 38 State Department employees, who were subordinates of Mrs. Clinton, for violations regarding her emails and concluded that "Clinton's use of private email had increased the vulnerability of classified information."

In October, 2014 the State Department requested Mrs. Clinton to send to the Department all of the emails related to official government work. Her lawyer, David Kendall, and her long-time State Department aide, Cheryl Mills, oversaw the review of the email archives in order to provide the work-related documents to the State Department. Through that process 30,000 emails were given to the State Department on December 5, 2014 and some 33,000 that were considered personal were not. To accomplish that sorting task Mr. Kendall and Ms. Mills would have to access the 22 Top Secret communications for which they held no security clearance.

On March 2, 2015 the New York Times published a story disclosing that Mrs. Clinton had used a personal email server while serving as Secretary of State.

On March 4, 2015 the Congressional Committee investigating the terrorist attack on the State Department offices in Benghazi, Libya, that killed a U.S. Ambassador and three other Americans, issued a subpoena requiring Mrs. Clinton to turn over all emails from her private server relating to the incident in Libya.

Between March 25-31, 2015 an employee of Platte River Networks, the private company hired by Mrs. Clinton to manage her email server, deleted the entire email archive using a software called BleechBit to ensure that any emails remaining on the private server could never be recovered.

On March 27, 2015 Mrs. Clinton's lawyers informed the Congressional Committee that had issued the subpoena for the emails, that all of the emails on her server relating to official government business had been turned over to the State Department on December 5, 2014.

On July 10, 2015 the FBI opened a criminal investigation into Hillary Clinton's handling of classified information while she was Secretary of State. The code name for the investigation was *'Midyear Exam'*. When FBI Director James Comey briefed Attorney General Loretta Lynch on the investigation he was asked to refer to the investigation as only a 'matter', not an investigation. Comey appointed FBI Agent Peter Strzok to head-up a team of FBI investigators who would proceed with looking into the investigation / matter. At the time that FBI Agent Peter Strzok was heading the Hillarygate email matter he was having an affair with FBI lawyer Lisa Page. He texted this note to Page: "God, Hillary should win 100,000,000 to 0."

In the course of the investigation Mrs. Clinton's long-time aide Cheryl Mills, who had overseen the sorting of the emails into the public and private categories, was invited to an interview by the FBI regarding the email matter. She granted the interview after the Justice Department granted her immunity. The employee of Platte River Networks, who deleted the entire email archive by using BleechBit, also granted the FBI an interview and was also given immunity.

On June 27, 2016 Attorney General Loretta Lynch held a 30-minute meeting with former President Bill Clinton inside her government airplane located on the tarmac of the Phoenix airport. When the press became aware of the meeting, she reported that nothing having to do with the email investigation was discussed. She explained that this was but a chance meeting and was simply a social discussion regarding grandchildren and hobbies of mutual interest. She then announced that, while there was no impropriety about the meeting whatsoever, in order to avoid any possible appearance of impropriety, she would then and there agree that she was simply going to accept the conclusion of FBI Director James Comey as the Attorney General's final conclusion to end the email matter once and for all. In essence, the policeman investigating a potential crime would make the prosecuting attorney's final decision of whether or not to proceed with a criminal indictment. Because that is contrary to established procedures of the Justice Department and the FBI, Acting Attorney General Rod Rosenstein would later recommend that FBI Director James Comey be fired for doing that.

Five days later, on July 2, 2016 Hillary Clinton was interviewed by the FBI team led by FBI Agent Peter Strzok. The meeting lasted 3 and ½ hours. The interview was voluntary. She was not under oath. No transcript or video recording was made. Only the notes of the FBI agents would be retained for the public record. Mrs. Clinton was accompanied by Cheryl Mills, acting as her attorney, as one of five lawyers representing Mrs. Clinton at the interview. Ms. Mills had served as Hillary Clinton's Chief of Staff at the State Department during the entirety of her service as Secretary of State. As such she would be a fact witness in the investigation. Normal FBI procedures would prevent a fact witness from serving as an attorney during Mrs. Clinton's interview.

Three days later, on July 5, 2016 FBI Director James Comey announced the FBI's findings at a press briefing. The FBI found that:

- Mrs. Clinton's lawyers had cleaned the email server "in such a way as to preclude forensic discovery."
- It was hard to understand how the sorting of emails into public and private categories was done because of the use of BleachBit but "we believe our investigation has been sufficient to give us reasonable confidence that there was no

intentional misconduct in connection with that sorting."

- "Although we did not find clear evidence that Secretary Clinton or her colleagues intended to violate the laws governing the handling of classified information, there is evidence that they were extremely careless in their handling of very sensitive highly classified information."

- "There is evidence to support a conclusion that any reasonable person in Secretary Clinton's position should have known that an unclassified system was no place for [Top Secret / Special Access Program Level] conversation."

FBI Director Comey then announced the FBI's conclusion regarding the Clinton email investigation / matter in this manner.

"Although there is evidence of potential violations of the statutes regarding the handling of classified information, our judgment is that **no reasonable prosecutor would bring such a case.** In looking back at our investigations into mishandling or removal of classified information, we cannot find a case that would support bringing criminal charges on these facts. All the cases prosecuted involved some combination of:

- clearly intentional and willful mishandling of classified information;

- or vast quantities of materials exposed in such a way as to support an inference of intentional misconduct;
- or indications of disloyalty to the United States;
- or efforts to obstruct justice.

We do not see those things here."

So, FBI Director Comey was recommending to the Attorney General that no criminal charges be brought and that the case be closed. Of course, that meant the case was in fact closed because the Attorney General had already announced that Comey would have the final say in the matter. It is interesting to note that in a May 2, 2016 email Director Comey distributed a draft of the statement that he would make two months later on July 5th. That Comey email was sent to FBI Deputy Director Andrew McCabe, General Counsel James Baker and Chief of Staff James Rybicki. On May 16th Rybicki sent a response email stating: "Please send me any comments on this statement so we may roll into a master doc for discussion with the Director at a future date. Thanks. Jim."

If the matter had been handled in the usual manner, whereby the police investigator does the investigation and turns over his findings to the prosecutor to make a final decision of whether or not to file criminal charges, things might have turned out differently. You see, the Justice Department prosecutors had quite recently prosecuted at least two Americans whose unlawful conduct was clearly not intentional and had a far-lesser consequence of harm to the security of our nation.

General David Petraeus was the commander of U.S. forces in Afghanistan in 2011. He kept highly classified materials in notebooks at his home at that time and shared them as background information with a biographer who was writing his biography. The biographer was a reserve military officer who held a clearance for handling classified materials but who had no formal authorization to review the specific information in the notebooks. The biographer signed an agreement that she would not write about classified information and the Pentagon later signed-off on the book's publication, agreeing that it contained no classified information. The biographer was never charged with a crime. FBI investigators wanted Petraeus to be charged with felony violations of the Espionage Act which bars unlawful communication of national defense information and retaining classified information without permission. The Justice Department crafted a plea deal and on March 3, 2015 Petraeus pled guilty to one misdemeanor crime of removing and retaining classified information, was fined $100,000, and placed on probation for two years.

Machinist Mate 1st Class Kristian Saucier was a 28-year-old, ten-year veteran of the U.S. Navy when he was convicted of a felony. After an FBI investigation of an incident that took place in 2011, he was prosecuted by the Justice Department in 2015 for sending cell phone snapshots of the interior of his submarine while at sea to his wife. You are not permitted to have a cell phone aboard a submarine. He was charged with espionage and initially pled not guilty. He was convicted, received a dishonorable discharge, and served a one-year prison sentence for the felony conviction.

In light of these two 2015 cases, perhaps Director Comey may have been wrong in drawing his conclusion that **no reasonable prosecutor would bring such a case.** However, the matter was moot at that point because of Attorney General Lynch's decision to defer the prosecution decision in this case to the FBI investigators. Time to move on. And, it just so happened that the end of Hillarygate allowed FBI Agent Peter Strzok to be available to take the lead on another case of great national importance.

The Watergate and Hillarygate scandals are over and done with. The facts are in. You can judge for yourself the extent, if any, of government corruption involved. Murphy would have found a lot of corruption in both scandals. She would be appalled by Republican corruption in the Watergate scandal and by Democrat corruption in the Hillarygate scandal. Let's move on to Russiagate.

Russiagate #1

The FBI has over 13,000 Special Agents. Peter Strzok was a very special one. He rose to become a Deputy Assistant Director of the Counterespionage Section and became a Deputy Assistant Director of the

Counterintelligence Division of the FBI. Strzok concluded his work as lead-investigator in the Clinton email matter known as *'Midyear Exam'* on July 5, 2016. On July 31, 2016 he was assigned by FBI Director James Comey to serve as the lead FBI agent conducting a new FBI counterespionage investigation called *'Crossfire Hurricane'*. That FBI probe was initiated to investigate Russian interference in the 2016 United States elections in collusion with the Trump presidential campaign. Any attempt to interfere with our fair and free elections must be prevented and parties who are found to have interfered must be prosecuted to the fullest extent of the law. Government investigators looking into such important matters must be completely objective and completely free of any partisan bias.

On August 8, 2016, eight days after Director Comey assigned Peter Strzok to be the lead investigator of *'Crossfire Hurricane'*, FBI Attorney Lisa Page texted Strzok asking: "[Trump's] not ever going to become President, right? Right?!" Strzok responded to the text: "No. No he's not. We'll stop it."

Eight days later Strzok sent the following text message to FBI Attorney Lisa Page: "I want to believe that the path you threw out in [former FBI Deputy Director Andrew McCabe's] office – that there is no way he gets elected – but I'm afraid we can't take the risk. It's like having an insurance policy in the unlikely event you die before you're 40." Clearly the person that he feels should never be elected is Donald Trump. In an earlier text he indicated that he thought Mrs. Clinton should be elected by the margin of 100,000,000 to 0.

The FBI counterintelligence investigation would continue to be focused on the collusion of Donald Trump and his campaign associates with the Russians to interfere in the 2016 election. Strzok would lead the investigation by the FBI for ten months until a Special Counsel was selected by Acting Attorney General Rod Rosenstein on May 17, 2017 to take over. If this seems a little confusing, that's because it is. Here is the background of what happened.

After Donald Trump was sworn into office as President on January 20, 2017, he appointed Jeff Sessions to be Attorney General in charge of the Justice Department. The FBI is an agency of the Justice Department. Sessions was confirmed by the Senate and assumed the duties of his office. On March 2, 2017 Sessions recused himself as Attorney General "from any existing or future investigations of any matters related in any way to the campaigns for President of the United States." Sessions had been a Trump campaign advisor and the scope of the FBI's 'Crossfire Hurricane' investigation included alleged collusion of Trump's campaign with Russia. He recused himself so there would be no hint of impropriety and Deputy Attorney General Rod Rosenstein was appointed Acting Attorney General to oversee the FBI's investigation of Trump campaign dealings with the Russians. Since the FBI was conducting that investigation Rosenstein would be in charge of overseeing the work of the FBI in that matter. James Comey was the Director of the FBI that was investigating the Trump campaign and Russia. On May 9, 2017 Acting Attorney General Rosenstein wrote a letter to President Trump recommending that Comey be fired. In his letter Rosenstein included this specific wrongdoing of Comey in conducting the Clinton email investigation / matter:

> "The Director was wrong to usurp the Attorney General's authority on July 5, 2016 and announce his conclusion that the case should be closed without prosecution. It is not the function of the Director to make such an announcement. At most, the Director should have said the FBI completed its investigation and presented its findings to federal prosecutors."

On May 10, 2017 President Trump fired FBI Director Comey.

On May 17, 2017 Acting Attorney General Rod Rosenstein appointed former FBI Director Robert Mueller to serve as Special Counsel to oversee the previously-confirmed FBI investigation of the Russian government's efforts to influence the 2016 election. In making the appointment Rosenstein provided this reasoning:

> "The public interest requires me to place this investigation under the authority of a person

who exercises a degree of independence from the normal chain of command."

Thus began the Mueller investigation that would continue for yet another 22 months. Peter Strzok would then join the staff of that independent Mueller investigation, but would be fired by Mueller when more emails showing his intense opposition and dislike of Trump came to light. The official Russiagate investigation then came to an end without finding any evidence of wrongdoing by Trump or his campaign. The professional counterintelligence investigation into Russiagate #1 had concluded. The political investigation by the Democrat-led House of Representatives would continue.

Russiagate #2

In May 2019 Attorney General Bill Barr appointed U.S. Attorney John Durham to open a criminal inquiry to investigate the origins of the Trump-Russia investigation and the conduct of the FBI, and the Intelligence Community during their deep-dive into possible connections between the Trump campaign and the Kremlin. Thus began Russiagate #2.

Russiagate #2 is a scandal of a different color. As of this writing it represents a case of potential government corruption by Democrats that may or may not be true. All the facts are not yet in. Because of that, Russiagate #2 should be considered only a story based on very incomplete facts. The incomplete facts, however, do present a non-fictional story of government corruption that involves Executive Agency Officials at the highest levels of government engaged in a biased and partisan Democrat effort to accomplish two things:

- First, to ensure that Donald Trump, the Republican candidate for President in 2016, would not get elected.
- Second, in the unlikely event that he did get elected, to ensure that he would first be rendered ineffective in performing the duties of the Office of President, and then be removed from that Office.

The story of the Russiagate #2 scandal involves not only high-level government officials. It also involves the cooperation and participation of members of the free press to assist the high-level government officials by publishing classified information that had been 'leaked' to them in an effort to damage Trump and his administration. The overarching story portrays an attempt to weaponize the American Justice system for political retribution. And that story should horrify every American.

The story is either fictional or non-fictional. The story is far from proven. What follows is the Russiagate #2 story based on the incomplete facts disclosed through public sources thus far. Each of us should draw our own conclusion based on facts and await final judgment until all the facts are in.

The first step of the story alleges that Democrat Executive Administrators at the highest levels of our

National Security Offices, including the National Security Agency, the CIA, the FBI, and the Attorney General's office, fabricated a tale that they felt would be highly effective against Donald Trump. The tale shows Trump and his campaign associates collaborating and colluding with the Russian government to steal the election away from Hillary Clinton by using the Russians to dig up dirt on Clinton and broadcast it in order to help Trump get elected. In essence, Donald Trump is actually an agent of the Russian government and a stooge of Vladimir Putin.

The second step of the story alleges that Democrat Executive Administrators at the highest levels of our National Security Offices engaged in coordinated efforts with Hillary Clinton's election campaign offices and the offices of the Democrat National Committee (DNC) to use a former British spy, Christopher Steele, to assemble a dossier of false information showing Donald Trump and his associates to be colluding with the Russians and detailing false lurid allegations about Trump's sexual perversions with Russian prostitutes. None of the information compiled in the dossier was true. But the Clinton campaign and the DNC were joined at the hip to ensure that Donald Trump would never be elected President. They funneled more than $160,000 through the Perkins Coie law firm to Christopher Steele for that false information. Christopher Steele had long-standing associations with the Justice Department and the FBI and he provided them with the false information in the dossier. Steele personally despised Donald Trump. That false information was then used as the primary basis for receiving a warrant from the Foreign Intelligence Security Act (FISA) court for the FBI to gain access to the email information and files of the Trump campaign (the modern equivalent of the Watergate telephone wiretaps). Our FBI never does stuff like this. The FBI has a well-deserved reputation for being a law enforcement agency of the highest repute. But this stuff was not done by average hard-working special agents. This stuff was done only at the highest levels of our National Security Offices.

The most damning part of the Russiagate #2 story alleges that evidence has been discovered that Executive Administrative Officials at the highest levels of our government used the powers of their offices to perpetrate a hoax on the American People that the incoming President was a Russian agent in an effort to remove him from office. And that these government officials would use the powers of their government offices in an attempt to tarnish the reputations and effectiveness of incoming members of the new administration by illegally leaking classified counterintelligence information to members of the press in order to accomplish that objective. And that they would use the awesome powers of the highest offices of the Intelligence Community, the FBI and the Justice Department to target political opponents in criminal investigations and entrap them into alleged felony crimes of perjury.

Whether the Russiagate #2 scandal is a true story or a fictional one will have to await the conclusion of U.S. Attorney John Durham's findings as he presents his report to Attorney General Barr and the American People.

Murphy kept informed by reading the *Fairmont Times* newspaper every day and watching the nightly news every evening. She usually preferred to watch NBC but she trusted the coverage of ABC and CBS as well. If she were alive today, she would decide to wait to make a verdict on Russiagate #2 until John Durham completes his investigation. She preferred to rely on facts instead of media spin.

CHAPTER 10

MURPHY'S VIEWS ON THE ROLE OF A FREE PRESS

The First Amendment of our Bill of Rights, contained in the United States Constitution, provides in part: "Congress shall make no law ... abridging the freedom of speech or of the press...." That amendment enshrined the principles that would allow the government of the United States to always be conducted under the close watch and critical eye of a free people. The government will not control the People. The People will control the government. Murphy simply said Amen to that.

A free and impartial news media has always been important to America. The press and news media are collectively called the Fourth Estate. The Fourth Estate functions best as a watchdog on the workings of government. The Fourth Estate has an unofficial but immense influence on public affairs of government. The Fourth Estate has the capacity to frame political issues and skew them to one side of the political spectrum or the other. The nation is best served when the news media is fair and impartial in its coverage of government. The free press has an obligation to always look at the work of government with a critical eye, to always be vigilant, but to always be fair. The American People rely on that kind of free press.

When Watergate became a national scandal in 1973 and led to the resignation of President Nixon, the independent press was instrumental in discovering and reporting the facts to a disbelieving nation. The foremost investigative reporters were Bob Woodward and Carl Bernstein of the Washington Post newspaper. Their editor, Ben Bradlee, insisted that their information be accurate and triple-sourced before it was reported. Primarily due to their coverage, the truth was ultimately revealed. The Washington Post reporters were awarded the prestigious Pulitzer Prize for Watergate coverage. Those were the good old days when stories were both accurate and objective and meticulously sourced. Editorials could be partisan in favor of one party or the other, but news stories like Watergate could not. Objective reporting served the public purpose.

As the Hillarygate and Russiagate #1 scandals began in 2016 and continued into 2020, the national news coverage by TV media as well as the most influential newspapers in the country, the New York Times and the Washington Post, did not perform the same role that the Washington Post had in Watergate. They chose sides and determined to skew media coverage to further the Democrat political agenda. Unsourced and misleading stories were presented as objective news even as they were known to be false. And, even after mistruths came to light, the reporters who pursued biased news stories with vigor were lauded for their efforts. The 2018 Pulitzer Prize was jointly awarded to the New York Times and the Washington Post for their reporting on national affairs with this citation:

> "For deeply sourced, relentlessly reported coverage in the public interest that dramatically furthered the nation's understanding of Russian interference in the 2016 election and its connections to the Trump campaign, the President-elect's transition team and his eventual administration."

After a 22-month investigation by Special Counsel Mueller, no such connections were ever discovered. But the Pulitzer Prize for 'relentless' reporting remained intact.

Murphy would have felt that biased news coverage, slanted to favor either the Republican Party or the Democratic Party, would be a travesty against the American People.

CHAPTER 11

MURPHY'S VIEWS ON PARTISAN POLITICS

Murphy thought that partisan politics was great. She loved political argument and rough and tumble politics. And she believed that having two strong political parties was a great thing for this country. The two opponents would battle hard for what they believed was right. And then they would sit down together to work out their differences in a compromise that would serve America best. There are two sides to every issue and neither side has the omnipotence to know the best solution to the problems facing our national community with absolute certainty. Such is the nature of being human. Compromise is the cornerstone for preserving the health and unity of our nation. That is what makes America great and the envy of the world. We do our best. Sometimes we fail. We try again to get it right.

Murphy would argue the merits of her position on issues with vigor. But she knew that she didn't have all the answers. She would be well-served by listening to the arguments of those who did not share her views. She would always learn something important by doing so. She taught me that.

The political arguments of government during Murphy's lifetime were not always polite and gentle. They were hardscrabble. Reaching agreement on major issues was never easy. It was a hard process. Real progress for the national community would be made only when both Democrats and Republicans craft legislation that both sides can agree on. Nobody ever gets everything that they want. An effective compromise must be crafted.

A French philosopher known as Voltaire was a major voice of the European Enlightenment and his ideas greatly influenced the founding of our nation. Our founders were guided by this adage attributed to Voltaire and found it to be quite useful in drafting our Constitution during the hot Philadelphia summer of 1787: "Perfection is the enemy of the possible." Before casting his vote in favor of the draft Constitution, an elderly Benjamin Franklin, made these remarks at the Constitutional Convention:

> "I confess that there are several parts of this constitution which I do not at present approve, but I am not sure I shall never approve them: For having lived long, I have experienced many instances of being obliged by better information, or fuller consideration, to change opinions even on important subjects, which I once thought right, but found to be otherwise. It is therefore that the older I grow, the more apt I am to doubt my own judgment, and to pay more respect to the judgment of others."

The problem facing the national community in the summer of 1787 was a daunting one. The politicians at the Constitutional Convention had to establish a framework for a national government that would provide for the very basis of our society and civilization, and that would last in perpetuity. That was a tall order. But they did it. And they did it by compromise. The overarching principle was the overall good of America. And they did their political job in less than four months using parchment and quill pens.

Franklin felt quite comfortable that the politicians drafting our Constitution had done a good job and was quite confident in America's future because of the work they had done and the compromises that they had made. George Washington presided over the Constitutional Convention sitting in an armchair with half-a-sun carved into its back. Eighty-one-year-old Benjamin Franklin remarked before signing the Constitution:

> "I have often looked at that behind the president without being able to tell whether it was rising or setting. But now I … know that it is a rising … sun."

I must admit that I never heard Murphy mention the Frenchman Voltaire. But she was a big fan of the wisdom of Ben Franklin. She strongly believed in the spirit of compromise that Franklin championed. And she saw that spirit in action in American politics during her lifetime.

In 1935, five years into the Great Depression, America was still experiencing 20% unemployment. Jobs programs were passed and major legislation was enacted to try and improve things. Some things did not work so we tried other things. The Democrats controlled both houses of Congress and FDR was President, but the landmark legislation that they enacted was not done in a partisan manner. The best example is the Social Security Act of 1935. In the House, Democrats voted 284 yes and 15 no. The Republicans voted 81 yes and 15 no. In the Senate the Democrat vote was 60 yes and 1 no. The Republican vote was 16 yes and 5 no.

In 1965 LBJ was President and Democrats controlled both houses of Congress. Again, landmark legislation was enacted in a non-partisan manner. The Medicare Act of 1965 was passed by a vote of 313 to 115. The Republican minority in the House cast 65 yes and 73 no votes. The majority Democrats voted 248 yes and 42 no. In the Senate 13 Republicans voted yes and 14 voted no, while the Democrat margin was 55 in favor and 7 against.

Landmark Civil Rights legislation was enacted by the same Congress. The Civil Rights Act of 1964 was passed by a non-partisan vote in both the House (290 to 130) and the Senate (73 to 27). The Voting Rights Act of 1965 was passed by a non-partisan vote of 333 to 85 in the House and 77 to 19 in the Senate. It is interesting to note that in fact a higher percentage of Republicans voted for these bills than Democrats. But that is not the real point. The point is that this landmark legislation would never have passed without bipartisan support. That is how our system is intended to work. Majority consensus built through compromise.

In 1970 the Clean Air Act, which enabled the creation of the Environmental Protection Agency, was signed into law by Republican President Richard Nixon. The legislation would not have passed without bipartisan support in the House with a yes vote by 67 Republicans and 206 Democrats. In 1973 the same President signed the Endangered Species Act with a vote of 390 to 12 in the House and 92 to 0 in the Senate. Majority consensus built through compromise.

Under the administrations of both Democrat and Republican Presidents, other landmark legislation has been enacted only with bipartisan support. Majority consensus built through compromise.

- The Interstate Highway Act of 1956
- The Economic Recovery Tax Act of 1981
- The Immigration Reform and Control Act of 1986
- The Fair Housing Act Amendments of 1988
- The Civil Rights Act of 1991
- The Personal Responsibility and Work Opportunity Act of 1996

Majority consensus built through compromise has largely been abandoned by our elected representatives in Congress during the last decade. That began in 2010 when it was decided by the Democrat President, the Democrat Speaker of the House and the Democrat Majority Leader of the Senate that compromise would no longer be necessary. If you held the Presidency and a sufficient majority in both Houses of Congress, landmark legislation could be passed without majority consensus through compromise. President Barack Obama was very clear about that as he stated: "Elections have consequences." In essence, my way or the highway.

The Affordable Care Act of 2010 was passed solely as a Democrat partisan act. The scope of the Act was gigantic. It would affect one-fifth of the entire American economy. The Act was signed into law by President Obama after it passed in the House by a vote of 219 to 212 and in the Senate by a vote of 60 to 39. **Not a single Republican member of Congress in either house voted in favor of the Affordable Care Act of 2010. Majority consensus built through compromise had been abandoned completely.**

Since the passage of that landmark legislation in 2010 the political atmosphere in our nation has become more and more partisan. Before then, members of both the Democrat and Republican parties had 'worked across the aisle' to forge solutions to the major problems facing our nation through compromise. Now, compromise had become a dirty world. It shows weakness. True Democrats must never compromise for they are convinced that their conception of truth, justice and the American way is the one and only way. The opposition must not be heard. The opposition party must simply be crushed by brute force. Members of the opposition party are not only wrong, they are bad, through and through. If they disagree, they are not just wrong, they are racist, sexist, homophobic, xenophobic and Islamophobic. Simply label them as evil people. Say it loud enough and often enough and it must be true. Republicans should never have been elected to political office and it is now the duty of true Democrats to remove them from office by any means possible. On November 3, 2016 Donald Trump was elected to serve as the 45th President of the United States of America. Before he was sworn into office on January 20, 2017, members of the United States Congress were calling for his impeachment and removal from office. The battle cry had been called. This was war. Take no prisoners.

Democrats have been very successful in many of the battles of the war that they announced. When they charged that Trump had been elected President only because he had collaborated with and been a puppet of Russian president Vladimir Putin, they were allegedly assisted by the efforts of partisan Executive Agency Officials at the highest levels of the FBI, the Justice Department, the CIA and the National Security Agency to find evidence of that charge. When the FBI counterintelligence investigation of Trump and his associates, led by Peter Strzok, turned up no such evidence, the Democrats were successful in calling for a further investigation of the matter by an Independent Counsel. The Mueller Investigation then did a deep dive into all matters Trump for 22 months, at a cost of over $30 million, to find the evidence of Trump collusion with Russia. The 17 lawyers working for Special Counsel Mueller on the case were all Democrats, and many were financial contributors to Hillary Clinton's presidential campaign, yet they found no evidence to support the charges. The official Mueller report concluded that neither Trump nor any of his associates were involved in any such collusion with Russia. But a battle had been won. The taint of the ongoing investigation was a great assist to the Democrats who thereby regained majority control of the House of Representatives in the 2018 mid-term election.

Now empowered with majority control of the House of Representatives, the Democrats launched a coordinated effort to impeach and remove Trump from office. They were undeterred when the Mueller report concluded that Trump and his associates were not guilty of any crimes. So, they turned to crimes that had to have been committed by Trump when he had a 30-minute telephone conversation with the newly-elected president of Ukraine on July 25, 2019. Trump released the full transcript of the phone call that he knew was monitored by many people within his administration. The Democrats used the phone call as incontrovertible evidence that Trump was collaborating with a foreign power, Ukraine, in order to help defeat his potential Democrat opponent in the upcoming 2020 election, Joe Biden. For this act Trump had to be impeached.

The Democrats sprang into action aggressively for they felt that leaving Trump in office until the November 2020 election would irreparably impair the nation. He simply had to be removed from office now for his crimes. Otherwise he might well get reelected. They elaborated that in that July 25th telephone call, President Trump had unlawfully solicited the Ukrainian authorities to influence the 2020 presidential election. The full transcript of the telephone call is readily available on the Internet. Read it for yourself and see if you believe that such an outlandish charge is justified.

The Democrats successfully Impeached President Trump on December 18, 2019 by adopting two Articles of Impeachment: Abuse of Power and Obstruction of Congress. Every single Republican in the House of Representatives voted against both Articles of Impeachment. After the House voted to impeach Trump the Speaker of the House, Nancy Pelosi, refused to send the Articles of Impeachment to the Senate to begin an Impeachment Trial for almost a month. During that time, she held the Articles of Impeachment hostage as she attempted to control the procedures of the Senate. On January 15, 2020 the Articles of Impeachment were presented to the Senate along with a 658-page impeachment report on the two charges. On February 5, 2020 all 47 Democrat Senators voted to convict Trump on both charges. One Republican Senator voted to convict Trump for Abuse of Power. No Republican Senator voted to convict Trump for Obstruction of Congress.

Progressive liberal Democrats today make no apologies for their approach and their methods. They make no apologies for they have come to believe that they, for the first time in history, possess the ability to discern what is right and what is best for all Americans. There is simply no room for compromise. They have somehow been endowed with the ability to know the final answer to all of the perplexing questions facing society. And, there is no room for argument. My way or the highway. They have a duty to right all the wrongs that they ascribe to the sins of America founded in a sinful beginning and perpetuated by a sinful nature of discrimination. To correct all past wrongs, they truly believe that our country must undergo fundamental change. Traditional institutions of society must be abandoned and replaced by a 'new normal', regardless of the consequences.

For 10,000 years of human history, the two-parent Family has been a bedrock foundation of civilization. Then in the United States, starting in the 1960s, that began to change. Progressive liberal Democrats, who today proclaim that they are 'woke', began to laud a different type of Family in America. The result has been amazing, and not in a good way. Worldwide an average of 7% of children under age 18 live in a single-parent household. In the United States the percentage is more than three times (23%) that number.

Today, Progressive liberal Democrats applaud the demise of the traditional Family and the rise of the 'new normal' belief that single-parent or same-sex parents are better able to raise children as they ought to be raised. They tell us that the conservative belief in the traditional Family, and traditional Family values, is the remnant of a capitalistic society that must be replaced by social democracy. The 'woke' generation has grown to believe that the Marxist path that they have been taught in school is the path that must be followed. As he harangued against the exploitative nature of capitalism, Karl Marx truly believed that the traditional Family was simply a tool of the evil capitalist, and must be destroyed.

As the Millennial Generation (1981-1996) came of age, the evidence continued to mount up. 57% of Millennial Moms are unmarried. 32% of Millennial Moms who have babies outside of marriage have four or more years of higher education. And they teach their children the values of the 'woke' approach that should be the 'new normal'.

For 10,000 years of human history, the traditional marriage of a man and a woman had been a bedrock foundation of civilization. Then in the United States, starting in the 1960s, that began to change. In 1965, 24% of Black babies and 3% of White babies were born to unwed mothers. In 2018, 70% of Black babies and 27% of White babies were born to unwed mothers. It is clear that the success of this Progressive Democrat approach has had an even more devastating effect on the families of the poor and disadvantaged.

Today the United States of America is the greatest country in the history of the world. This country is the only country in the history of the world that fought a civil war to end the institution of slavery. This country is the only country in the history of the world that won a war and then rebuilt the enemy's country and economy and then departed. We did that twice in the last century. This country is the land of freedom and opportunity and the hope of the world. People throughout the world who want freedom and opportunity want to live in the United States of America.

This country is not a perfect country. We have problems in our society. We always have and we always will. As a People we have good hearts and good intentions. When we make mistakes, we admit them and strive to do better. That is the way of freedom and opportunity for all. That can only be done by our political system of representative democracy through compromise. That is the American way.

Our country simply cannot survive if the path of raw partisan politics now pursued by the Democratic Party continues to be followed. The end result of raw partisan politics is anarchy followed by authoritarian government. One side wins and the other side loses. Permanently. Dissent will no longer be allowed. Dissent is evil and the good of the country requires that opposing views of what has been determined to be right and pure and proper cannot be abided. We have seen this story played out on the world stage before with the raw power wielded by socialist and communist leaders. The outcome has always been disastrous as freedom and liberty have been abandoned in the name of security. Some say that cannot happen in America. I fear that is simply wishful thinking. We see evidence on our college campuses that dissent is only permitted in 'free speech zones'. And our children are now taught a version of history that portrays our great nation as stained at birth and evil throughout in the treatment of the poor and disadvantaged in our society. Partisan politics and a 'one size fits all' solution to societal issues is not the path of the Republican Party. That is the path of the Democrats.

Our Constitution requires the President of the United States to annually report on the 'State of the Union'. By tradition this requirement is met through a speech by the President to a joint assembly of both houses of Congress. The speech is televised and watched by millions of Americans and people throughout the world. The Speaker of the House of Representatives, Nancy Pelosi, invited President Donald Trump to make his annual 'State of the Union' address on February 4, 2020. At the conclusion of President Trump's 'State of the Union' address, the television cameras captured the image for the American People and the world of Speaker Pelosi standing behind the President and ripping a copy of his 'State of the Union' message into shreds, again, and again, and again.

So, what would Murphy have felt about all of this exercise of blatant partisan politics. She would have abhorred it. That simply is not how our government should conduct business.

CHAPTER 12

MURPHY'S VIEWS ON RACISM

Slavery is despicable. Since civilization began 10,000 years ago until about 200 years ago, slavery was the norm of society. That is an awful truth. But that is a truth. In this country our society was torn apart by the issue of slavery. From 1861 to 1865 a great Civil War was fought to rid the nation of slavery. More Americans died fighting that great Civil War than in all the other American wars put together. Slavery is the epitome of racism. My great, great grandfather died in battle fighting for the Union to rid the country of slavery. His Commander-in-Chief was Republican President Abraham Lincoln.

When the Declaration of Independence was signed in 1776 and the Constitution was ratified in 1788, racism was a compelling force in American society. Institutional slavery of Black Americans was widespread. White people actually 'owned' Black people. Many of our legendary founding fathers owned Black slaves. It is hard to get more racist than that. But it is always important to not judge by today's standards and mores the standards and mores of life that existed two and one-half centuries ago. At that time the institution of slavery had been a continuous part of western civilization for ten thousand years.

Our White, male founders were aware of the evil presented by the institution of slavery and that slavery of Blacks presented a glaring contradiction to the founders' stated belief that 'all men are created equal'. Many founders wanted to abolish slavery at that time but recognized that the standards and mores of the times would have prevented the fledgling country from ever getting started if they insisted on abolition concurrent with passage of the Constitution. A clause was included in the Constitution that prevented Congress from passing a law that would prohibit the importation for slaves into the country for 20 years. And it is important to note that on the exact date first allowed, Congress passed a law prohibiting the importation of slaves. They knew that slavery was evil and many wanted to abolish it.

American society was torn apart by the issue of slavery for more than 50 years after the passage of that law. The Republican Party was founded in 1854 in the struggle to rid society of that evil. President Abraham Lincoln was elected as the first Republican President in 1860, signed the Emancipation Proclamation in 1863 and was the Commander-in-Chief of the federal forces as they fought the Confederacy to win the Civil War in 1865.

After President Lincoln was assassinated in that year, it was the Republicans who carried out Lincoln's dream and secured passage of the 13th, 14th, and 15th Amendments to the Constitution to guarantee that slavery was abolished for all time and that free Black

Americans were provided with due process of the laws and equal protection of the laws, and guaranteed the right to vote. Republicans were the prime movers for the passage of those amendments. They were opposed by Democrats. And, lest we forget, Democrats were the party of the Confederacy and slavery.

The Democrats remained the sustainers of racial hatred and discrimination in this country long after the end of the Civil War. Democrats controlled the political machines in the Southern states and enacted 'Jim Crow' laws that discriminated against Blacks and resulted in segregated schools, neighborhoods, restaurants, rest rooms, drinking fountains and buses. Democrat President Woodrow Wilson praised the KKK and opposed passage of a federal anti-lynching law. FDR also opposed a federal anti-lynching law and made racially discriminatory and segregationist policies and practices an integral part of the 'New Deal' of the 1930s.

Reverend Martin Luther King, Jr. led the Civil Rights movement of the 1960s to rid the nation of segregation and to ensure the integrity of the Black vote. The Civil Rights Act of 1964 and the Voting Rights Act of 1965 were passed into law through the leadership of Democrat President Lyndon Baines Johnson. Those acts were the bipartisan efforts of Democrats and Republicans alike. The fact is that a higher percentage of Republican members of both the House of Representatives and the Senate voted for those two laws than did their Democratic colleagues. Those two landmark pieces of legislation virtually ended government-enforced racial discrimination in America. Forced busing was implemented to integrate public schools, affirmative action was implemented in colleges and universities, racial discrimination in housing or commerce or transportation was illegal. President Johnson then implemented a War on Poverty and launched the Great Society. He believed that Progressive Liberals could implement programs to bring an end to racial injustice and poverty in America's great cities. As LBJ eloquently stated, our great cities would be:

> "…a place where every child can find knowledge to enrich his mind and enlarge his talent…where the city of man serves not only the needs of the body and the demands of commerce but the desire for beauty and the hunger for community."

Progressive liberals had concluded that the mission of government had less to do with ensuring economic fairness and more to do with helping the poor and disadvantaged find meaning in their lives and achieving a level of spiritual happiness. And they aggressively embarked on ambitious projects to provide public housing and good schools and social programs to achieve that mission. And that is the path that they have continued on for the past fifty years. During that time the Democrat Party has been in control of our great cities. Literally trillions of taxpayer dollars have been invested to do that for all that time. The results have been dismal. Yet, White Progressive Democrats continue to promise that they will take care of the poor and disadvantaged minority Americans living in those great cities if they simply allow them to do so by voting them into office again and again so that they may continue to increase government assistance. And at the Federal government level, they have been quite successful in securing the minority vote by doing that.

Over the past fifty years White Progressive Democrats have portrayed themselves as the champions and protectors of the poor and disadvantaged minorities in America's great cities. They have engaged in the hard work of securing taxpayers' money to provide an increasing amount of dependency on government for the poor and disadvantaged in those cities. That represents institutional racism implemented by White Progressive Democrats founded on the assumption that poor and disadvantaged minority Americans simply cannot succeed without government help supplied by caring White Progressive Democrats. Minority Americans who are poor and disadvantaged are no different than anyone else. They want the true opportunity to succeed by securing the dignity of work through a good job, and the promise of a good future for their children, by securing a good education for them in a school of their own choosing.

At one time in our nation's history White Democrats exploited poor and disadvantaged minorities for their labor through slavery. Today they exploit them for their votes. That is racism.

Murphy and my Mother taught me that any form of racism is despicable. Every person is a gift from God and is possessed of unique individual talents. Every person is entitled to be treated with dignity and respect. Everyone is free and equal under the law to pursue happiness as they see fit. There is no place in American society for racism.

CHAPTER 13

MURPHY'S VIEW ON POLITICAL RACISM

As of this writing there is widespread outrage in America about the murder of an unarmed Black man while handcuffed by a White Police officer. The Police officer killed George Floyd by crushing his neck with his knee for over eight minutes while three other Police officers stood by and watched without stopping the murder. I do not know anyone in the country that is not outraged by that egregious act of violence. That unconscionable act of violence has now been used by radicals as the justification for defunding or actually eliminating Police departments, which would prove disastrous for minority communities. And it serves as the justification for the assertion that all White Americans are somehow guilty by association for George Floyd's murder unless they acknowledge that their white privilege and silent support of systemic racism in America is the cause of his death. That is absolutely absurd. Murphy opposed racism in any form. I oppose racism in any form. And I resent being called a racist simply because I am White. Being born White was not a choice that I made. Working in the coal mines to pay my way through college was not some form of White privilege. My Black coal miner friend, Jessie Smith, would have agreed with that.

The banner of righteousness that has been raised by White Progressive Democrats is to now embrace White guilt as the answer to make things better. Apparently, if Whites just acknowledge that they have collectively harmed Black and Hispanic Americans by racial prejudice injustice that has always been endemic in our country, then things will get better for the minorities that have been harmed by that prejudice. Well, that all sounds quite noble. What it is in fact is meaningless. What is meaningful and far more useful is for White Americans to work hard with the disadvantaged and poor of the minority communities to eliminate the barriers that are holding Black and Hispanic Americans back from realizing the American dream. A hand-up instead of a hand-out. Provide a good job with fair pay to raise a good family and happiness will follow. That has always been the effective American way for Italians, Poles, Jews, Asians, and even the descendants of the Irish coal miners. It will continue to be the effective American way for African American Blacks and Hispanics. Nothing will ever be as effective as supporting the dignity of the individual through hard work. History has clearly shown that the most effective method of reducing poverty of the poor and disadvantaged is through market capitalism.

Reverend Al Sharpton has been a vocal advocate of civil rights for minorities for many decades in this country. At the memorial service held for George Floyd in Minneapolis on June 4, 2020 Reverend Sharpton made this pronouncement:

"George Floyd's story is the story of Black folks. You kept your knee on our neck. We had creative skills, but we couldn't get your knee off our neck. It's time for us in George's name to stand up and say, 'Get your knee off our necks.' We don't want favors, just get up off of us, and we can be and do whatever we can be."

The unconscionable murder of George Floyd by a Police officer is used by Reverend Sharpton as proof that Blacks must rise up and force White people to recognize their collective White guilt and stop White people from oppressing Black people any further.

That is a powerful message to the African American Black community. And that message is a message of political racism. In essence, White Americans have always oppressed Black Americans and that oppression has prevented Black Americans from being successful in America. That is a powerful message that all White people are guilty of systemic racism in America. White people must get their collective knee off the necks of Black Americans and allow Blacks to finally succeed.

Is that powerful message actually true?

Regardless of race or ethnicity the two things that Americans are concerned with the most are: the safety of their family; and the education of their children. And these are concerns that are primarily addressed in local communities. Elected Mayors and City Councils decide what tax dollars are to be provided for public safety and what processes and procedures are to be used by the police department. Elected members of the School Board decide what tax dollars are to be provided for public school education and what processes and procedures are to be used to provide the best public education possible for their children. Elected prosecutors and elected judges administer the system of criminal justice in the local community. Who elects all of these public officials? They are elected by the People who live in the local community. So, what is my point?

Reverend Sharpton's claim is not supported by the facts. Facts are hard. But facts are facts. The Black and Hispanic electorates in our great American cities have held an overwhelming electoral advantage over Whites for a long time. That electoral advantage over Whites put these cities under the political control of Democrats for a long time. These are facts concerning the racial and ethnic percentage make-up of many of the major American cities where poor and disadvantaged minority Americans live. U.S. Census Bureau data as of July 1, 2019 is provided on the next page.

U.S. Census Bureau Data, July 1, 2019

CITY	WHITE	BLACK	HISPANIC	OTHER
New York City	32.1%	24.3%	29.1%	14.5%
Chicago	32.8%	30.1%	29.0%	8.1%
Los Angeles	28.5%	8.9%	48.6%	14.0%
Detroit	10.3%	78.6%	7.6%	3.5%
Washington, DC	36.2%	46.9%	10.9%	6.0%
Atlanta	37.6%	51.8%	4.3%	6.3%
Philadelphia	34.6%	42.3%	14.5%	8.6%
Baltimore	27.5%	62.5%	5.1%	4.9%
New Orleans	30.6%	59.7%	5.5%	4.2%
Cleveland	33.7%	49.6%	11.6%	5.1%
Birmingham	23.4%	70.5%	3.7%	2.4%
Memphis	25.7%	64.2%	7.2%	2.9%

Each of these major American cities has a strong Democrat Mayor serving as chief executive. The political decisions of these great cities have been largely controlled by elected Democrat officials, Mayors, City Council Members, School Board Members, Prosecutors and Judges for roughly the past 50 years. The Black and Hispanic voters, comprising an overwhelming majority of the population of these communities, have voted for the politicians who have developed and implemented the policies and procedures that have led to the deplorable living conditions for the poor and disadvantaged in these cities. The voters have continued to believe the promise of change offered by Democrats even as Democrat elected officials perpetuate the status quo by barring Charter School choice and increasing government assistance in order for the poor and disadvantaged to continue to be able to live a life without the dignity of a good job and independence from government. That is simply wrong. The Democrat approach to solving the problems of the poor and disadvantaged minorities of our great cities simply has not worked. It may have been well-intended at one time, but it has been proven not to work.

Progressive liberal Democrats who are White have been very successful in convincing a lot of disadvantaged and poor Black Americans that they truly care about them. In truth, they have been very successful in convincing the leading Black officials in these great American cities that they would help keep them in office by providing more and more Federal dollars for the poor and disadvantaged to be spent in their communities. And those Federal dollars have largely been used to keep those Black officials in office to maintain the status quo of government dependency and poverty.

Progressive liberal Democrats who are White completely agree with Reverend Sharpton. Whites bear the burden of a collective racial guilt and must atone for their sins. Blacks have been the victims of Whites who have rigged the system against minorities. The solution is to now tear the existing system down and build a new system that is based on social justice for minorities. An economic system based on capitalism and free enterprise must be replaced by an economic system founded on socialism. They promise the minority community that no one needs to work unless they want to. And because they acknowledge their collective White guilt, the 'woke' Progressives will work hard to provide minorities with all they need for a happy life. After all, members of the minority community are simply the victims of White oppression and deserve to be cared for by Progressive White Democrats.

The first step toward the accomplishment of this goal is to protest in the streets of our great American cities. The protests will show the solidarity needed to accomplish this worthy goal. The burning and looting and destruction of the neighborhoods of the poor and disadvantaged in these cities will be viewed as a small price to pay for the accomplishment of the social justice needed. The thousands and thousands of 'woke' White Progressive Democrats who join the movement promise to join with the poor and disadvantaged minorities to accomplish the goal. Collective righteousness is on the march.

Conservative Republicans who are White completely disagree with that approach. The Republican approach is in actuality a more caring and effective approach.

What White Americans like myself propose is to actually help the poor and disadvantaged minority citizens living in our great American cities by offering a hand up. That help will be in the form of the Federal government working with the private sector to bring good jobs and opportunities to those citizens. That help will be in the form of convincing the elected officials of those great cities to allow the children of the poor and disadvantaged minority citizens to attend Charter Schools where they can get a decent education. That help will be in the form of working with the elected officials of those great cities to develop government work programs to help rebuild the municipal infrastructure and eliminate housing slums. That help will be done not by a handout but by hard work for which the workers receive fair pay. And those public jobs programs will be ended when the work is done and the workers have gained the skills necessary to gain good employment in the private sector of our economy. That help will be in the form of implementing actual reform of our criminal justice and prison system that will provide equitable sentences for crimes committed and an actual path of rehabilitation for citizens who have made mistakes to become productive members of society upon returning to their community from prison life. That help will be done by eliminating burdensome licensing requirements so that it is possible to actually operate a thriving business out of the home and to let child care be provided by other caring folks who happen to live down the block.

These are the things that the current President of the United States, Donald Trump, has not only proposed but is actually doing and is determined to implement. The biggest successes so far are the First Step Act for Prison Reform, the start of Opportunity Zones and an Apprenticeship Program. These things are done not by replacing an economic system based on free enterprise and capitalism. These things are done by embracing that economic system and using it to provide real opportunity for the poor and disadvantaged minority citizens living in our great cities.

Like everyone on this Earth, Donald Trump is a flawed human being. He says things that I find to be appalling. He calls people names. He engages in trivial and petty acts as he occupies the office of President and is the leader of the free world. I sincerely wish he did not do those things. But he does. For me that presents a dilemma. And I know that would present a dilemma for Murphy. Should I refuse to vote for Donald Trump because of these things? Or should I vote for him because the policies and programs that he supports are the exact ones that I support in order to provide the best pursuit of a happy life of freedom and liberty and prosperity for every American? Unlike today's elected Democrat leaders, I will not duck the issue by voting 'Present'. I will either vote Yes or No. My choice is to vote Yes. I will vote for Trump and I will vote for the Republicans who support the same policies and programs that he supports. By volumes, actions speak louder than words.

Murphy would yell at Donald Trump: "Clean up your act!!" Then Murphy would vote for him.

CHAPTER 14

BREAKING MURPHY'S PROMISE

Murphy wanted me to always be a Democrat. To ensure that, she specifically asked me to promise that I would always be registered to vote as a Democrat. I made that promise not once, but twice.

I do not make promises lightly. It is very important to me to keep promises.

I have been a registered Democrat for all of my adult life, more than 50 years. This week I will be breaking Murphy's Promise by changing my voter registration from Democrat to Republican. I am doing so in the sincere belief that she would want me to do so.

In 1974, the year that Murphy departed this Earth, the Democratic Party was a far different party than the party that it has become today.

I truly believe that if Murphy were alive today, she would be a registered Republican. That party now represents the values that she believed in and cherished.

I am certain that the intent of Murphy's Promise was that I uphold the values that she believed in and cherished. And I fully intend to do so. I simply cannot do that as a Democrat. What Democrat officials of our government have done during the last decade is anathema to everything that I believe in and everything that Murphy believed in.

If Murphy were alive today, she would be ashamed to be a Democrat. I am ashamed to be a Democrat. And I will never be one again.

The only way that I can actually keep Murphy's Promise is by Breaking Murphy's Promise. And Murphy would be proud of me for doing that.

I am not suggesting by this book that anyone else should share my views. Each of us is a proud American citizen who has been blessed by God to live in the greatest country on Earth. Each of us now has the liberty as free individuals to examine the actual facts, to express their own views, and to vote their own conscience. May that always remain true.

This book was written for one person and one person only – Murphy. Murphy loved America. I love America. I love Murphy. God bless America and God bless you Grandma.